Karl Breul

A handy bibliographical guide to the study of the German language

and literature for the use of students and teachers of German

Karl Breul

A handy bibliographical guide to the study of the German language and literature for the use of students and teachers of German

ISBN/EAN: 9783337204914

Printed in Europe, USA, Canada, Australia, Japan

Cover: Foto ©Paul-Georg Meister /pixelio.de

More available books at **www.hansebooks.com**

ᴺDY BIBLIOGRAPHICAL GUIDE

TO THE STUDY OF THE

ᴺ LANGUAGE AND LITERATURE

A HANDY*

BIBLIOGRAPHICAL GUIDE

TO THE STUDY OF THE

GERMAN LANGUAGE

AND

LITERATURE

FOR THE USE OF

STUDENTS AND TEACHERS OF GERMAN

COMPILED AND EDITED

(*With two Appendices and full Indexes*)

BY

KARL BREUL, M.A., Ph.D.

CAMBRIDGE UNIVERSITY LECTURER IN GERMAN; EXAMINER IN GERMAN
TO THE UNIVERSITY OF LONDON; LATE EXAMINER TO THE
UNIVERSITIES OF CAMBRIDGE, OXFORD, AND TO
THE VICTORIA UNIVERSITY

HACHETTE AND COMPANY

LONDON: 18 KING WILLIAM STREET, CHARING CROSS
PARIS: 79 BOULEVARD SAINT-GERMAIN
BOSTON : CARL SCHOENHOF
1895

Edinburgh: T. and A. CONSTABLE, Printers to Her Majesty

PREFACE

THE present book has been written in the first instance
to meet the wants of English students of German, but it
is hoped that it will also prove useful to teachers who
wish to continue their reading,[1] and who are unable
to obtain advice as to what books to use. Librarians
of Colleges wishing to provide the most necessary
books for the study of German may be materially
helped in their selection by referring to this Guide.
Although written expressly for the use of *English*
students, the book may also prove useful to the ever-
increasing class of Continental and American students
who are devoting themselves to the scientific study of
the German language and literature. They will, no
doubt, have to add to and to omit from the lists given
on the following pages, but the greater part of the
Guide will be of service to students and teachers of no
matter what nationality. Students who are anxious
to take up any special branch of German philology

[1] With regard to the necessary self-training of Modern Language
teachers, see my lecture to the College of Preceptors 'On the
Training of Teachers of Modern Foreign Languages,' printed in the
Educational Times of May 1st, 1894. The number may be bought
separately.

should first work through the books mentioned in the
Guide ; in so doing they will come across many references to other works.

In writing this Guide, my aim has been to supply
students and teachers with the titles of the *most
important* periodicals and books. Instead of aiming
at bibliographical completeness, I wished to offer
a selection of such books as are still really useful.
˙Hence the present is not by any means a book like
E. Hübner's excellent handbooks on the Latin Language
and Literature, for, however useful these are to advanced
students, yet they far exceed the wants of beginners.
Nor is this Guide intended to be a mere supplement to
K. v. Bahder's more comprehensive work called ' Die
deutsche Philologie im Grundriss,' Paderborn, 1883,
which is written on a totally different plan. Advanced
students and scholars will in all cases have to consult
v. Bahder's Grundriss, Paul's Grundriss, the various
' Jahresberichte' recording the progress of German
philology and literature, and the other bibliographical
helps enumerated in § III. But it is hoped that not
many books of real importance for ordinary students
have been overlooked, and that in every case the best
books of reference have been mentioned. Whoever
makes a selection of books is liable to be criticised for
admitting certain books and omitting others, and it
is impossible to please everybody. But I shall at all
times be very grateful if scholars using this book will

kindly point out to me any omissions, or will let me
have any hints and corrections suggested by their
experience.

In order not to make the Handy Guide too bulky
and too expensive, I have purposely omitted all articles
from periodicals and also those which are contained
in collected writings mentioned in this book. Thus,
for instance, K. Burdach's excellent investigations
into the language of Goethe's early writings and the
history of the German literary language which have been
published in various periodicals; O. Jänicke's valuable
supplementary notes to K. Müllenhoff's 'Zeugnisse
und Excurse zur deutschen Heldensage' (in HZ. xv.);
W. Wackernagel's admirable 'Geschichte des deutschen
Dramas bis zum Anfang des 17. Jahrhunderts' (Kl.
Schr. ii. 69 *sqq.*); F. Holthausen's instructive essay on
the development of the German ballad (ZZ. xv.);
and many others, have been intentionally omitted.
The only exception to this rule is the special mention
of some articles from Paul's 'Grundriss der germanischen Philologie.' I have permitted myself some
other slight inconsistencies in order to enhance the
practical usefulness of the book for English students.
Such inconsistencies are the enumeration of certain
classics and of certain annotated editions, and the
omission of others which have equal claims to be
mentioned. For instance, editions of Hartmann v.
Aue's 'Iwein' and Wolfram v. Eschenbach's 'Parzival'

have been mentioned, while the epics of Heinrich
v. Veldegge and Gottfried v. Strassburg are omitted.
But as 'Iwein' and 'Parzival' are the two most
important M.H.G. epics of their kind, and as they
are studied before all others at our Universities, they
had to be specially mentioned. Such old classics as
are frequently set for University examinations here and
elsewhere, *e.g.* Otfrid, Tatian, Walther, Nibelunge,
Kudrun, Reinke, Hans Sachs, have also been included. Again, in order to save space, only some of the
principal books on the history of the Novel, of Lyrics,
and of the Drama have been given—for the history
of the less important branches of literature, such as
the Fable, etc., v. Bahder's work should be consulted.
With one or two exceptions, none but English and
German periodicals are given, and many important old
periodicals and collections published in Germany, such
as Grimms' 'Altdeutsche Wälder'; Hagen, Docen und
Büsching's 'Museum für altdeutsche Litteratur und
Kunst'; Hoffmann's 'Findlinge' and 'Fundgruben';
Mone's 'Quellen und Forschungen'—have been omitted
from the Guide. Nothing that is now quite superseded,
however great its historical importance, has been inserted,
but books which contain some chapters still worth
reading have not been excluded. This will account
for the rejection of Bopp's, and for the admission of
Schleicher's, Compendium. Sometimes the purely logi-
cal arrangement has been set aside for the sake of con-

venience, *e.g.* the book. on German familiar quotations
cannot strictly be classed under the head of 'Language
and Grammar.' The Indexes will easily set every-
thing right.

I hope that this little Guide, which is more concise
and contains more recent information than v. Bahder's
excellent Grundriss, will be acceptable to many students.
It will also save lecturers, at least to some extent, the
irksome duty of reading out titles. The scientific value
or the special use of various books on the same subject
should be discussed by the teacher in his lectures.
In order to help those students who have no opportunity
of consulting a teacher, I have prefixed to a certain
number of books the letters *a*, *b*, *c*, *p*. The books
marked *a* will be found to be specially useful for more
advanced students; those marked *b* are intended for
beginners, who ought to possess the most important of
them. The symbol *p* is used to indicate books written
in a popular style and addressed to a somewhat wider
circle of readers; while *c* means that caution is necessary in using the books so marked, because they are
either partly superseded, or because the theories ex-
pounded in them are not yet well enough established
or generally accepted. Thus books like W. Scherer's
'Geschichte der deutschen Sprache,' or E. Sievers'
'Altgermanische Metrik,' have been marked *ac*. I
trust these symbols will be found useful, though I
freely admit that some scholars will in certain cases

differ from me with regard to the symbol to be prefixed. In my lectures I give of course much fuller information concerning such books, and also on certain
set authors and works, *e.g.* Walther von der Vogelweide
and Goethe's 'Faust,' than could be conveniently given
in a general guide such as this.[1]

I have as far as possible given the dates of the latest
editions. The indexes will, I hope, be found useful in
more than one respect. Under the system of arrangement adopted in the book, works on special authors, *e.g.*
on Goethe, are mentioned in different places, but such
books will be found collected under one heading in the
Index of Subjects. Again, the names of all the scholars
whose works appear in the Guide are given in alphabetical order in the Index of Authors. In arranging
the list the modification of vowels has been disregarded,
thus *a, ä, ae* have been treated alike. The lists of
abbreviations and symbols will be of use to many
beginners; the desirability of such helps has been
frequently brought home to me.

---

[1] Some still more general works, in which German Grammars,
Dictionaries, and annotated editions of classics have been enumer-
ated, are the following: (1) *A Classified Catalogue of Educational
Works.* London: Sampson Low, Marston, Searle and Rivington,
1887, pp. 136-144. (2) W. S. Sonnenschein, *The Best Books.*
London, 1891. (In various places.) (3) *A Guide-Book to Books.*
Edited by E. B. Sargant and Bernhard Whishaw. London: H.
Frowde, 1891. ('German Language and Literature,' pp. 149-160,
by H. J. Wolstenholme.) See also my article in the *ZfdU.* viii.
(1894), 167 *sqq.*

Blank pages at the end of the book have been given
to · enable students to add titles of books which are
not mentioned in the Guide, or which are published
subsequently.

If this Handy Guide should meet with a favourable
reception, I may be encouraged to prepare a companion
volume on the study of the English Language and
Literature.

In conclusion, I wish to tender my heartiest thanks
to my friend Dr. Wilhelm Seelmann, of Berlin, who has
most kindly assisted me with many valuable suggestions
while the proofs were passing through the press.

K. B.

ENGLEMERE,
    CAMBRIDGE,
        Christmas, 1894.

CONTENTS

I.

PERIODICAL PUBLICATIONS.

*Zeitschrift für deutsches Alterthum und deutsche Litteratur, started by **Moritz Haupt** under the title 'Zeitschrift für deutsches Alterthum,' Leipzig, 1841, and continued after Haupt's death (1873) by **Karl Müllenhoff** and **Elias Steinmeyer.** In 1876 the old title was changed into the present one, and **Wilhelm Scherer** joined the staff of editors. The principal editor was **Elias Steinmeyer,** and after the death of Müllenhoff (1882) and Scherer (1886) the periodical was edited by him alone. Since 1890 it has been edited by **Edward Schroeder** and **Gustav Roethe.** Berlin, Weidmann. Vol. XXXVIII., 1894.

Quarterly. Yearly one volume. Contains only original articles, mostly concerning the older stages of the Germanic languages and their literature. There is an index at the end of the later volumes.

[Abbrev. : **ZfdA.** or **HZ.** (= **Haupt's Zeitschrift**) ; in the periodical itself only **Zs.**]

A

*Anzeiger für deutsches Alterthum und deutsche Litteratur. Contains only reviews of recent scientific books and essays, and was started in 1876. Forms part of the 'Zeitschrift,' has its own pagination and cannot be bought separately. Vol. XX. Berlin, Weidmann, 1894.
[Abbrev. : **AfdA.**, and in the Zeitschrift only : **Anz.**]

*†Germania. Vierteljahrsschrift für deutsche Alterthumskunde, started by **Franz Pfeiffer.** Stuttgart, 1856. Continued by **K. Bartsch,** at first with the help of **J. Strobl,** and edited after Bartsch's death (1888) by **O. Behaghel.** Vol. XXXVII. Wien, 1892.
Quarterly. Yearly one volume. Original articles. Reviews. Very valuable Bibliography. Discontinued after 1892.
[Abbrev. : **Pfeiffer's Germ.**, or usually **Germ.**]

†Germanistische Studien, a supplement to the preceding, was edited by **Karl Bartsch.** Wien, Vol. I. (1872). Vol. II. (1875).
[Abbrev. :—**Germ. Stud.**]

*Zeitschrift für deutsche Philologie, started by **Ernst Höpfner** and **Julius Zacher.** The latter was the principal editor. Halle, 1868. It was continued after Zacher's death (1890) by **Hugo Gering** and **Oskar Erdmann.** Vol. XXVII. 1894.
Quarterly. Yearly one volume. Original articles and reviews. The original articles treat mostly of older German literature. Complete index of contents at the end of each volume. A supplementary volume (Ergänzungsband) was published in 1874.
[Abbrev. :—**ZfdPh., Zs. fdph.,** or **ZZ.** (=**Zacher's Zeitschrift.**)]

*Beiträge zur Geschichte der deutschen Sprache und Litteratur, started by **Hermann Paul** and **Wilhelm Braune,** 1874. Continued (with the assistance of Paul and Braune) by **Eduard Sievers.** Vol. XIX., Halle, 1894. There is an index to Vols. I.-XII. Three times a year. Yearly one volume. Only. original articles on the older German and Germanic languages and literatures. No Reviews and no bibliography.

[Abbrev.:—**Beitr.** or **P.B.B.** or, rarely, **B.P.B.**(= **Beiträge von Paul und Braune.**]

†Archiv für die Geschichte deutscher Sprache und Dichtung, edited by **Joseph Maria Wagner.** Vol. I. (the only one). Wien, 1874.

Zeitschrift für die deutsche Sprache, edited in 1887 by **Daniel Sanders.** Vol. I. Hamburg, 1888. Later volumes : Paderborn. Yearly 12 parts.

*Jahrbuch des Vereins für niederdeutsche Sprachforschung, started in 1875 by **August Lübben** and others. Vol. XIX. Norden, 1894. The present editor is **Wilhelm Seelmann.** Yearly. Miscellaneous contributions to the study of the Low German language and literature in all their stages.

[Abbrev.:—**Ndd. Jb.** (=**Niederdeutsches Jahrbuch.**)]

Korrespondenzblatt des Vereins für niederdeutsche Sprachforschung. Hamburg, since 1877. Every second month. Small communications. Notes and Queries.

†Alsatia. Jahrbuch für Elsässische Geschichte, Sage, Alterthumskunde, Sitte, Sprache und Kunst, edited by August Stöber. Mühlhausen, 1851-76.

Alemannia. Zeitschrift für Sprache, Litteratur und Volkskunde des Elsasses und Oberrheins, now : Zeitschrift für Sprache, Kunst und Alterthum, besonders des schwäbisch-alemannischen Gebietes. Started by Anton Birlinger, now edited by Friedrich Pfaff. Bonn. Since 1873. Vol. XXII. 1894.

> Contains many articles which have nothing to do with the language and literature of South-West Germany.

Strassburger Studien. Zeitschrift für Geschichte, Sprache und Litteratur des Elsasses, edited by Ernst Martin and W. Wiegand. Strassburg. Since 1883.

†Die deutschen Mundarten, started by J. A. Pangkofer, subsequently edited by Karl Frommann. 6 volumes. Nürnberg (subsequently Nördlingen), 1853-9.

ι   In 1877-8 one more volume was published (Halle), but no more followed.

Bayerns Mundarten. Beiträge zur deutschen Sprach- und Volkskunde, edited by O. Brenner and A. Hartmann. München. Since 1892.

---

*†Weimarisches Jahrbuch für deutsche Sprache, Litteratur und Kunst, edited by H. A. Hoffmann von Fallersleben and Oskar Schade. 6 vols. Hannover, 1854-7.

> Most of the essays concern German literature after 1500 and popular customs.

[Abbrev. :—Weim. Jahrb.]

†Jahrbuch für Litteraturgeschichte, edited by
Richard Gosche. Vol. I. (the only one), Berlin, 1865. A
continuation of this periodical was the following :

*†Archiv für Litteraturgeschichte, started by Richard
Gosche, Leipzig, 1870. Continued until 1887 by Franz
Schnorr von Carolsfeld. Vol. XV. is the last one. Leip-
zig, 1887.
> Quarterly. Every year one volume. Original articles and
> reviews chiefly concerning Modern German literature. In-
> dex at the end of each volume.
> [Abbrev. :—Archiv or AfLG. or Schnorr's Archiv.]

*†Vierteljahrschrift für Litteraturgeschichte, with
the assistance of Erich Schmidt and B. Suphan, edited
by B. Seuffert. Weimar, 1888-93. 6 vols. 1893.
> Quarterly. Yearly one volume. It was intended to take
> the place of AfLG. Discontinued after 1893. Index at
> the end of each volume.

*Euphorion. Zeitschrift für Litteraturgeschichte,
edited by August Sauer. Bamberg, 1894.
> This quarterly periodical is intended to be a sort of con-
> tinuation of the Vierteljahrschrift. It is principally
> devoted to the study of Modern German literature without
> excluding articles on Old German or on foreign literature.

†Vierteljahrsschrift für Kultur und Litteratur der
Renaissance, edited by Ludwig Geiger. Vol. I.
Leipzig, 1886. Vol. II. Berlin, 1887.

*Zeitschrift für vergleichende Litteraturge-
schichte, edited by Max Koch. Vol. I. Berlin, 1887.

In the following year this periodical and the preceding one
were combined under the title : **Zeitschrift für vergleichende Litteraturgeschichte und Renaissance-
Litteratur, Neue Folge,** edited by **Max Koch** and
Ludwig Geiger. Vol. I. Berlin, 1887-88. Vol. IV. Berlin,
1891. Since then the periodical was continued under the old
title **Zeitschrift für vergleichende Litteraturgeschichte,**
edited by **Max Koch.** Berlin, 1892. Vol. VII. (neue
Folge I.), 1894.
Every second month.
[Abbrev. :—**Z. f. vgl. Litt. Gesch.**]

†**Akademische Blätter,** started by **Otto Sievers.** Braunschweig, 1884.
One Volume. Modern German Literature.

*****Goethe Jahrbuch,** edited by **Ludwig Geiger.** Frankfurt
am Main, since 1880. Vol. XV., 1894. An elaborate
general Index to Vols. I-X. Frankfurt am Main, 1889.
Yearly. Original articles. Full account of all writings,
etc. concerning Goethe and his works. Index at the end of
most volumes.
[Abbrev. :—**GJ.**, or in the periodical itself **Jahrb.**]

Schriften der Goethe Gesellschaft. Vols. I.-IX.
Weimar, 1885-94.
Editions of valuable documents nearly all concerning
Goethe's Life and Writings, most of which had not been
printed before.

Publications of the English Goethe Society, London.
Published for the Society by David Nutt. 1886-1893.
5 Vols.
Containing Transactions, Original Papers, Translations, etc.

Transactions of the Manchester Goethe Society, 1886-1893. Being Original Papers and Summaries of Papers read before the Society, to which is added a classified catalogue of the Society's library. Warrington, 1894.

Zeitschrift für den deutschen Unterricht, edited by **Otto Lyon,** with the assistance of **Rudolf Hildebrand.** Vols. I.-VIII. (and 3 **Ergänzungshefte**). Leipzig, 1887-94. Monthly. Yearly one volume. Chiefly for teachers. [Abbrev. :—**Zs. f. d. d. Unt.** or **ZfddU.**]

*Archiv für das Studium der neueren Sprachen und Litteraturen, started by **Ludwig Herrig.** Braunschweig, since 1846. Continued after Herrig's death (1889) by **Stephan Waetzoldt** and **Julius Zupitza.** Vol. 92. 1894.
Quarterly. Original essays and reviews. Includes German, English, French, Italian, and other books. Chiefly for teachers.
[Abbrev. :—**Herrig's Archiv** or **Arch. f. n. Spr.**]

Die neueren Sprachen. Zeitschrift für den neusprachlichen Unterricht, mit einem Beiblatt 'Phonetische Studien,' started and edited by **Wilhelm Vietor.** Marburg i/H. Since 1893. Yearly ten parts. Vietor is the general editor and is assisted by **Franz Dörr** and **Adolf Rambeau.**

Revue de l'enseignement des langues vivantes, edited by **A. Wolfromm.** Paris. Since 1883.

†Internationale Zeitschrift für allgemeine Sprachwissenschaft. Started and edited by F. Techmer
Vols. I.-V. and one supplementary volume. Leipzig,
1884-90.

†Phonetische Studien. Zeitschrift für wissenschaft-
liche und praktische Phonetik, mit besonderer Rücksicht auf die Reform des Sprachunterrichts. Started
and edited by Wilhelm Vietor. Marburg. Since 1888.
6 Vols. Discontinued as such in 1892. Forms now part of
Vietor's new periodical 'Die Neueren Sprachen.' Cf. p. 7.

†Zeitschrift für die Wissenschaft der Sprache,
edited by Albert Höfer. Vols. I.-IV. Berlin, 1845-50.
Greifswald, 1851-53.

*Zeitschrift für vergleichende Sprachforschung
auf dem Gebiete der indogermanischen Sprachen,
started by Adalbert Kuhn, now edited by E. Kuhn and
Joh. Schmidt. Berlin, since 1852. (Vol. XXI. = Neue
Folge I.). Vol. XXXIII. Gütersloh, 1894.
[Abbrev. :—Kuhn's Zs. or KZ. or Z.f.vgl.Spr.]
Contains many important contributions to the study of
Germanic philology from a comparative point of view.

*Beiträge zur Kunde der indogermanischen Spra-
chen, started by Adalbert Bezzenberger, now edited by
A. Bezzenberger and W. Prellwitz. Göttingen. Since
1877.
[Abbrev.:—BB. or Bezzenberger's Beitr.]
Contents similar to those mentioned above.

*Indogermanische Forschungen. Zeitschrift für in-
dogermanische Sprach- und Altertumskunde, herausgegeben von Karl Brugmann und Wilhelm Streitberg.
With a 'Beiblatt': Anzeiger für indogermanische Sprach-
und Altertumskunde, ed. W. Streitberg. Strassburg.
Since 1891. Vol. IV. 1894.

Revue de linguistique et de philologie comparée.
Recueil trimestriel. Since 1867. Paris. Vol. XXVI.
1893.

---

†Zeitschrift für deutsche Mythologie und Sitten-
kunde, started by J. W. Wolf, continued by W. Mannhardt. Göttingen, 1853-59.

†Zeitschrift für Völkerpsychologie und Sprach-
wissenschaft, herausgegeben von M. Lazarus und H.
Steinthal. Berlin. Vols. I.-XX. Berlin, 1860-1890.
[Abbrev. :—Z. f. Völkerpsych.]

Zeitschrift des Vereins für Volkskunde, im Auftrage
des Vereins herausgegeben von Karl Weinhold. Berlin.
Vol. I. 1891. Vol. III. 1893.
    This new periodical is intended to take the place of the
before-mentioned Z. f. Völkerpsychologie.

---

*Göttingische gelehrte Anzeigen, unter der Aufsicht
der Königlichen Gesellschaft der Wissenschaften.
Göttingen. Since 1753.
    [Abbrev. :—GGA. or Gött. gel. Anz.] Detailed Re-
views.

†Anzeiger für Kunde der deutschen Vorzeit.
Neue Folge. Organ des germanischen Museums. Vols.
1-30. Nürnberg, 1853-83. The older title of this periodical
was : Anzeiger für Kunde des deutschen Mittelalters.
Eine Monatsschrift, edited by Freiherr von Aufsess (subsequently by F. J. Mone). Years I.-VIII. Nürnberg,
1832. Karlsruhe, 1839.

†Jenaer Litteraturzeitung, im Auftrage der Universität Jena herausgegeben von A. Klette. Jahrgang
I. Jena, 1874. Vol. VI. Leipzig, 1879.

*Litterarisches Centralblatt für Deutschland,
started by Friedrich Zarncke, now edited by Ed.
Zarncke. Leipzig. Since 1850.
[Abbrev. :—LCB.] Weekly. Short Reviews. Bibliography and Contents of Magazines and Periodicals.

*Deutsche Litteraturzeitung, Kritische Rundschau
über die gesammten Wissenschaften, started by Max
Roediger, continued by August Fresenius, and now
edited by Paul Hinneberg. Berlin. Since 1880.
Weekly. Short reviews of books concerning all scientific
subjects. Bibliography and at first Contents of Periodicals.
[Abbrev. :—DLZ. or D. Litt. Zeit.]

*Revue Critique d'histoire et de littérature. Paris.
Since 1866. The present editor is A. Chuquet.

*Litteraturblatt für germanische und romanische
Philologie, started and edited (originally with collabora-
tion of K. Bartsch) by O. Behaghel and Fr. Neumann.
Heilbronn, 1880. Vol. XV. Leipzig, 1894.
Monthly. Short reviews. Enumerates all the books,

articles, notes published separately or in magazines, periodicals, newspapers concerning the scientific study of Germanic
and Romance philology and literature. Most useful to
teachers.

[Abbrev. :—Litt. Bl., or LB. fgurPh.]

Bibliotheca Philologica oder geordnete Uebersicht
aller auf dem Gebiete der classischen Alterthumswissenschaft wie der ältern und neueren Sprachwissenschaft in Deutschland und dem Auslande neu
erschienenen Bücher. Göttingen. Since 1848. Since
1885 edited by **A. Blau.** Half-yearly.

*Jahresberichte über die Erscheinungen auf dem
Gebiete der germanischen Philologie, heraus-
gegeben von der Gesellschaft für deutsche Philologie in
Berlin. The contributors are **Gotth. Bötticher, Joh.
Bolte, Aloys Brandl, M. Hartmann, Emil Henrici,
Karl Kinzel, Wilh. Seelmann,** and others. Vol. I. (works
and articles published in 1879). Berlin, 1880. Vol. XIV.
(1892), 1893.

Yearly a volume. Full indexes. Easy survey of all the
books, pamphlets and articles concerning the German and
cognate languages and German literature up to the 16th
century (inclusively).

*Jahresberichte für neuere deutsche Littera-
turgeschichte, herausgegeben von **Julius Elias, Max
Hermann, Siegfried Szamatólski.** Vol. I. (treating of
the works published in 1890). Stuttgart, 1892. Vol. II.
(year 1891). 1893.

Yearly a volume. Full indexes. Easy survey of the vast
modern literature.

Berichte des Freien Deutschen Hochstiftes zu Frankfurt am Main. Quarterly. Part of these consist of 'Litterarische Mitteilungen. Neuere Goethe- und Schillerlitteratur' (by **Max Koch**). No. IX. 1894.

Jahres-Verzeichniss der an den deutschen Universitäten erschienenen Schriften. Vol. I. (^{15}viii. 1885—^{14}viii. 1886). Berlin, 1886. The last volume is Vol. IX. (1893-4). Berlin, 1894. An Index to Vols. I.-V. arranged according to subjects was published in 1891. Official survey.

Jahres-Verzeichniss der an den deutschen Schulanstalten erschienenen Abhandlungen. Vol. I. (year 1889). Berlin, 1890. Vol. V. (1893). Berlin, 1894. Official survey.

Bibliographischer Monatsbericht über neu erschienene Schul- und Universitätsschriften. (Dissertationen—Programmabhandlungen—Habilitationsschriften, etc.). Herausgegeben von der Centralstelle für Dissertationen und Programme von **G. Fock**. Leipzig. Part I. 1889-90. Part IV. 1892-93.

Yearly 12 parts, affording an easy survey of recent pamphlets. Special Index to Vol. IV. (and foll.).

The Athenæum. Journal of English and foreign Literature, Science, the Fine Arts, Music and the Drama. London. Since 1828.

It appears weekly and contains reviews and short original articles.

The Academy. A weekly review of Literature, Science, and Art, since 1869. It contains reviews and short original articles.

Notes and Queries. A medium of intercommunication for literary men, artists, antiquarians, genealogists, etc. London. Since 1850. The last volume published is Vol. IV. of the Eighth Series. 1893. Published in weekly parts.

Transactions of the Philological Society. London. Since 1842. From 1842-53 the periodical was called 'Proceedings of the Philological Society'; in 1854 the present title was assumed.

American Journal of Philology. Edited by **Basil L. Gildersleeve.** Baltimore. Since 1880. Vol. XV. 1894.

Modern Language Notes. Baltimore. Vol. I., 1886. Vol. IX. (1894), in progress. The editors are **A. Marshall Elliott, James W. Bright, Hans C. G. v. Jagemann, Henry Alfred Todd.**

Eight numbers a year. Reviews and original articles.

Modern Languages. The organ of the Modern Language Association. Edited by **J. J. Beuzemaker.** Vol. I., No. 1. London, 1894.

Publications of the Modern Languages Association of America, edited by **James W. Bright.** Baltimore. Since 1884. The 9th volume is in course of publication.

Sitzungsberichte der Berliner (Wiener, Münchener, etc.) **Akademie der Wissenschaften,** published periodically and containing very valuable contributions. The articles respecting Germanic and German Philology and Literature are contained in the 'Philosophisch-historische Klasse.'

For important **Dutch** and **Scandinavian Periodicals** cp. Paul's Grundriss der germanischen Philologie I., 104-105.

II.

SERIES OF ESSAYS AND COLLECTED WRITINGS.

A. BY VARIOUS AUTHORS.

†Mittheilungen der deutschen Gesellschaft zur Erforschung vaterländischer Sprache und Alterthümer in Leipzig. 8 vols. Leipzig, 1856-90.

Quellen und Forschungen zur Sprach- und Cultur-geschichte der germanischen Völker. Edited by Bernhard ten Brink, Wilhelm Scherer, and Ernst Martin. Strassburg. Since 1874.
Many valuable treatises on grammar and literature.
[Abbrev.:—QF.]

Germanistische Abhandlungen, started by Karl Wein-hold, now edited by Fr. Vogt. Vols. I.-X. Breslau, 1882-94.

Acta Germanica. Organ für deutsche Philologie, ed. by Rud. Henning and Jul. Hoffory. Vols. I.-III. Berlin, 1889-91.

Schriften zur germanischen Philologie, edited by Max Roediger. Helft, I.-VI. Berlin, 1888-91.

Berliner Beiträge zur germanischen und roma-nischen Philologie, edited by Emil Ebering. Berlin, 1893-94.

14

**Forschungen herausgegeben vom Verein für nie-
derdeutsche Sprachforschung.** Vols. I., II., V.,
VI. have appeared. Leipzig and Norden, 1886-93.
ᴵAbbrev.:—Ndd. Forschungen.]

Theatergeschichtliche Forschungen, ed. Berthold
Litzmann. Parts I.-VIII. Hamburg. (Interesting for the
general history of German Literature.)

Beiträge zur deutschen Philologie, a single volume,
dedicated to Julius Zacher by various scholars. Halle,
1880.

Altdeutsche Studien, von Oskar Jänicke, El. Steinmeyer,
and Wilh. Wilmanns. Berlin, 1871.

Studien zur Litteraturgeschichte, Michael Bernays
gewidmet von Schülern und Freunden. Hamburg, 1893.

Festschriften für Rudolf Hildebrand. (a) Forschun-
gen zur deutschen Philologie. Leipzig, 1894. ed. K.
Burdach. (b) Festschrift zum siebzigsten Geburtstage
Rudolf Hildebrands. . . . ed. O. Lyon. (Ergänzungsheft
zum achten Jahrgange der Zeitschrift für den deutschen
Unterricht.) Leipzig, 1894.

B. BY ONE AUTHOR.

Jacob Grimm. Kleinere Schriften. 8 volumes. Gütersloh,
1864-1890.

Jacob Grimm. Auswahl aus den Kleineren Schriften.
Berlin, 1871, ²1875.

Wilhelm Grimm. Kleinere Schriften. 4 volumes. Gütersloh, 1881-87.

Wilhelm Wackernagel. Kleinere Schriften. 3 volumes. Leipzig, 1872-74. (Vol. I. : zur deutschen Alterthumskunde und Kunstgeschichte. Vol. II. : zur deutschen Literaturgeschichte. Vol. III. : zur Sprachkunde) (ed. by M. Heyne).

Ludwig Uhland. Schriften zur Geschichte der Dichtung und Sage. 8 volumes. Stuttgart, 1865-73. (Edited by L. Holland, A. v. Keller, and Fr. Pfeiffer).

Franz Pfeiffer. Freie Forschung. Kleine Schriften zur Geschichte der deutschen Litteratur und Sprache. Wien, 1867.

Karl Lachmann. Kleinere Schriften. Vol. I. : K. S. zur deutschen Philologie (ed. by Karl Müllenhoff). Berlin, 1876.

Wilhelm Scherer. Kleine Schriften. Edited by Konrad Burdach and Erich Schmidt. 2 volumes. Berlin, 1893.

Wilhelm Scherer. Vorträge und Aufsätze zur Geschichte des geistigen Lebens in Deutschland und Oesterreich. Berlin, 1874.

Heinrich Rückert. Kleinere Schriften. (Edited by Am. Sohr and Al. Reifferscheid.) 2 vols. Weimar, 1877.

Karl Bartsch. Gesammelte Vorträge und Aufsätze. Freiburg und Tübingen, 1883.

Hermann Hettner. Kleine Schriften. Edited by A. Hettner. Braunschweig, 1884.

Rudolf von Raumer. Gesammelte sprachwissenschaftliche Schriften. Frankfurt am Main and Erlangen, 1863.

R. H. Hiecke. Gesammelte Aufsätze zur deutschen Litteratur (edited by O. Wendt). Second (unchanged) edition. Berlin, 1885.

Erich Schmidt. Charakteristiken. Berlin, 1886.

Karl Lucae. Aus deutscher Sprach- und Litteraturgeschichte. Gesammelte Vorträge. (Edited by Max Koch.) Marburg, 1889.

Rudolf Hildebrand. Gesammelte Aufsätze und Vorträge zur deutschen Philologie und zum deutschen Unterricht. Leipzig, 1890.

III.

GERMANIC AND GERMAN PHILOLOGY.

Wilhelm Scherer. Jacob Grimm. Berlin, 1865 ; ²1885.

[a] **Rudolf v. Raumer.** Geschichte der germanischen Philologie, vorzugsweise in Deutschland. München, 1870. [Geschichte der Wissenschaften in Deutschland. Neuere Zeit. Vol. IX.]

[b] **Friedrich Pfaff.** Romantik und Germanische Philologie. Heidelberg, 1886. A University lecture.

[c] **Hermann Paul.** Geschichte der germanischen Philologie, in Paul's Grundriss. Vol. I. Strassburg, 1891.

H. Hoffmann v. Fallersleben. Die deutsche Philologie im Grundriss, ein Leitfaden zu Vorlesungen. Breslau, 1836.

> To a great extent superseded by v. Bahder's work, but not quite incorporated in it. A good bibliographical survey of the older literature on the subject.

K. H. Herrmann. Bibliotheca Germanica. Verzeichnis der vom Jahre 1830 bis Ende 1875 in Deutschland

18

erschienenen Schriften über altdeutsche Sprache und Litteratur nebst verwandten Fächern. 1 volume. Halle, 1878.
Valuable in spite of many inaccuracies.

[a] **Karl v. Bahder.** Die deutsche Philologie im Grund-riss. Paderborn, 1883. Bibliographical only. Excluding the works on single authors. Indispensable for scholars.

[a] **Hermann Paul.** Grundriss der germanischen Phi-lologie. Strassburg, Vol. I., 1891. Vol. II. (with a full Index), 1893. This is a fundamental work, compiled by many first-rate specialists. It contains numerous valuable bibliographical references, and is indispensable for scholars.

Yearly Records of the Progress of Germanic and German Philology and the Study of German Literature.

a. Jahresberichte über die Erscheinungen auf dem Gebiete der germanischen Philologie. Since 1879. Cf. p. 11.

b. Jahresberichte für neuere deutsche Litteraturgeschichte. Since 1890. Cf. p. 11, and the articles and reviews contained in several of the Periodicals which are enumerated under I., especially the 'Litteraturblatt für germanische und romanische Philologie.' Cf. p. 10.

IV.

LANGUAGE.

A.—THE SCIENCE OF LANGUAGE AND INDO-GERMANIC PHILOLOGY.

[bc] **John Peile.** Philology. London, [4]1880.

[bc] **F. Max Müller.** Lectures on the Science of Language. London, 1861. Last edition. London, 1891. 2 vols.

[bc] **A. H. Sayce.** Introduction to the Science of Language. London, 1880. 2 vols.

W. D. Whitney. Life and Growth of Language. International Scientific Series. Vol. 16. London, 1875. This book was translated into German by **August Leskien,** under the title 'Leben und Wachsthum der Sprache.' Leipzig, 1876.

W. D. Whitney. Language and its study, with special reference to the Indo-European family of languages. Seven lectures. New York, 1867. Edited in an abbreviated form with Introduction, Notes, etc., by **R. Morris.** London, 1876, [4]1884. There is a German translation with additions by **Julius Jolly.** München, 1874.

20

Otto Jespersen. Progress in Language, with special reference to English. London, 1894.
Contains several chapters which will be useful to students of German.

b **Berthold Delbrück.** Einleitung in das Sprachstudium. Ein Beitrag zur Geschichte und Methodik der vergleichenden Sprachforschung. Leipzig, 1880, ³1893.

b **B. Delbrück.** Das Sprachstudium auf den deutschen Universitäten. Praktische Ratschläge für Studierende der Philologie. Jena, 1875.

ac **Wilhelm v. Humboldt.** Über die Verschiedenheiten des menschlichen Sprachbaues. Herausgegeben und erläutert von **A. F. Pott.** 2 vols. Berlin, 1875. New edition, with Introduction and additions by **A. F. Pott,** and with various Indexes by **A. Vanicek.** 2 vols. Berlin, 1880.

a **G. v. der Gabelentz.** Die Sprachwissenschaft, ihre Aufgaben, Methoden und bisherigen Ergebnisse. Leipzig, 1891.

a **Hermann Paul.** Principien der Sprachgeschichte. 1880, ²1886. [English translation by **H. A. Strong,** London, 1888. 2nd ed. 1891.]

h **H. A. Strong, W. S. Logeman and B. J. Wheeler.** Introduction to the Study of the History of Language. London and New York, 1891. English adaptation—not a translation—of the former.

P. v. Bradtke. Über Methode und Ergebnisse der arischen Alterthumswissenschaft. Giessen, 1889.

ᵃ **Otto Schrader.** Sprachvergleichung und Urgeschichte.
Jena, ¹1883, ²1890. The second edition has been entirely
rewritten and considerably enlarged. It has been translated
into English under the title, 'Prehistoric Antiquities of
the Aryan Peoples,' by **Frank Byron Jevons.** London,
1890.

ᵇ **Otto Schrader.** Ueber den Gedanken einer Kulturgeschichte der Indogermanen auf sprachwissenschaft-
licher Grundlage. Jena, 1887.

Victor Hehn. Kulturpflanzen und Hausthiere in ihrem
Uebergang aus Asien nach Griechenland und Italien,
sowie in das übrige Europa. Historisch-linguistische
Skizzen. Berlin, ⁶1894 (edited by O. Schrader with botanical
contributions by A. Engler). There is an English translation of this work under the title, 'The Wanderings of Plants
and Animals from their first Home,' by **James Steven
Stallybrass.** London, 1885, ²1888.

Gustav Meyer. Essays und Studien zur Sprachgeschichte und Volkskunde. Vol. I., Berlin, 1885. Vol II.
Strassburg, 1893.

ᵇ **Hermann Osthoff.** Das physiologische und psycho-
logische Moment in der sprachlichen Formenbildung.
Berlin, 1879.

August Fick. Die ehemalige Spracheinheit der Indogermanen Europas. Göttingen, 1873.

ᵇ **Johannes Schmidt.** Die Verwandtschaftsverhält-
nisse der indogermanischen Sprachen. Weimar, 1872.

Karl Penka. Die Herkunft der Arier. Wien, 1886.

P **G. H. Rendall.** The Cradle of the Aryans. London, 1889. ●

P **Isaac Taylor.** The Origin of the Aryans. An account of the prehistoric ethnology and civilisation of Europe. Illustrated. London, 1890.

Johannes Schmidt. Die Urheimath der Indogermanen und das europäische Zahlensystem. Berlin, 1890.

Theodor Benfey. Geschichte der Sprachwissenschaft und orientalischen Philologie in Deutschland seit dem Anfange des 19. Jahrhunderts mit einem Rückblick auf die früheren Zeiten. München, 1869. [Geschichte der Wissenschaften in Deutschland. Neuere Zeit. Vol. VIII.]

ac **August Schleicher.** Compendium der vergleichenden Grammatik der indogermanischen Sprachen. 4th ed. Weimar, 1876. Contains very much that is now superseded, but is still of value for advanced students. It contains only Phonology and Morphology, but no Syntax. There is a translation of Part I. by **Herbert Bendall.** London, 1874.

a **Fritz Bechtel.** Die Hauptprobleme der indogermanischen Lautlehre seit Schleicher. Göttingen, 1891.

ac **Karl Brugmann.** Grundriss der vergleichenden Grammatik der indogermanischen Sprachen. I. (Introduction and Phonology). Strassburg, 1886. II. (Word-formation and Inflexion). Strassburg, 1889-1892. Detailed Indexes to this work, compiled by the author, were published in 1893 ; and **Berthold Delbrück** is adding a third volume, treating of the Comparative Syntax of the Indogermanic Languages. The first half of this third part was published in 1893. The title of the English translation is ' Elements of

the Comparative Grammar of the Indogermanic Languages.'
Vol. I. (1888), by **J. Wright** ; Vols. II. (1891), Vol. III.
(1892), and Vol. IV. (1894), by **R. S. Conway** and **W. H.
D. Rouse.** Note that the last volume (IV.) of the English
translation contains many corrections of Vol. I. of which the
author is preparing a second edition. An Introduction to
the Study of Indogermanic philology and especially to
Brugmann's Grundriss is being prepared by **Wilhelm Streitberg** under the title, 'Die indogermanische Sprachwissenschaft. Ihre Methode, Probleme, Geschichte.' Strassburg.

ac **August Fick.** Vergleichendes Wörterbuch der indo-
germanischen Sprachen, sprachgeschichtlich angeord-
net. *Third* edition. Göttingen. Vol. I. (1874) contains
'Indogermanische Grundsprache, arische und europäische
Spracheinheit'; Vol. II. (1876), 'Graeco-Italisch, Letto-
Slavisch, Prusso-Lettisch'; Vol. III. (1874), 'Die Germanische Spracheinheit' (with a 'Begleitwort' by Adalbert
Bezzenberger); Vol. IV. (1876), 'Nachwort und Indices.'
The *fourth* edition is now in course of publication. It is
edited by Adalbert Bezzenberger, August Fick, and Whitley
Stokes. Part I., Göttingen, 1890. Part II., Göttingen,
1894. The first part (by Fick) contains, beside a valuable
introduction, the originally Indogermanic, the Aryan, and the
West-European words. The second (by **Whitley Stokes**
and **A. Bezzenberger**) contains the originally Celtic words.

B.—PHONETICS.

b **Henry Sweet.** A Primer of Phonetics. Oxford, 1890.

b **Laura Soames.** An Introduction to Phonetics. London,
1891.

Ernst Brücke. Grundzüge der Physiologie und Syste-
matik der Sprachlaute. Für Linguisten und Taub-
stummenlehrer. Wien, 1856, ²1876.

[a] **M. Trautmann.** Die Sprachlaute im allgemeinen
und die Laute des Englischen, Französischen und
Deutschen im besonderen. Leipzig, 1884-86.

Eduard Sievers. Grundzüge der Phonetik, zur Einführung in das Studium der Lautlehre der indogermanischen Sprachen. Leipzig, 1876, ⁴1893.

Eduard Sievers. Phonetik. In Paul's Grundriss, I. 266-
399.

In the two last-mentioned works, especially in the first,
a very useful bibliography of the subject is given.

[a] **F. Techmer.** Phonetik. Zur vergleichenden Physiologie der Stimme und Sprache. Part I. : Die akusti-
schen Ausdrucksbewegungen. Leipzig, 1880. Part II.:
Illustrations.

Johan Storm. Englische Philologie. Anleitung zum
wissenschaftlichen Studium der englischen Sprache.
Vom Verfasser für das deutsche Publikum bearbeitet.
Part I. Heilbronn, 1881. The first portion of the second
edition, completely re-written and very considerably enlarged, appeared at Leipzig in 1892, under the title 'Die
lebende Sprache. 1.· Phonetik und Aussprache.' The
second portion of Vol. I. has been announced for 1895.

In this valuable book the theories of old and modern
phonetists have been thoroughly discussed.

The older books of **A. M. Bell** and **A. J. Ellis** are quoted
in full and discussed by Sievers and by Storm.

O. Bremer.   Deutsche Phonetik.   (Sammlung kurzer Grammatiken deutscher Mundarten.   Vol. I.).   Leipzig, 1893.

Phonetics have been and are being carefully investigated by many scholars in ' Vietor's Phonetische Studien,' and 'Die neueren Sprachen,' and 'Techmer's Internationale Zeitschrift für allgemeine Sprachwissenschaft.'   Cf. under **Periodicals,** pages 7 and 8.

V.

GERMAN LANGUAGE AND GRAMMAR.

HISTORICAL GERMAN GRAMMAR AND HISTORY OF THE GERMAN LANGUAGE.

ac **Jacob Grimm. Deutsche Grammatik.** 4 vols. (I. 1819,
²1822, a thoroughly revised edition of the first half (vowels)
in 1840, of the whole (according to Grimm's own copy of
the edition of 1822) with some slight improvements in 1870
(by W. Scherer); II. 1826, ²1878 (**by** W. Scherer); III.
1831, ²1889-90 (by G. Roethe and E. Schroeder); IV. 1837.)
An index to this work was compiled by **K. G. Andresen.**
Göttingen, 1865. (**GG.** or simply **Gramm.**)

ac **Jacob Grimm. Geschichte der deutschen Sprache.**
¹Berlin, 1848. 2 vols. ⁴Leipzig, 1880. 1 vol. (**GDS.**)

ac **Wilhelm Scherer. Zur Geschichte der deutschen
Sprache.** Berlin, ¹1868, ²1878. Reprint of the second
edition in 1890. (**GDS.**)

ac **Adolf Holtzmann. Altdeutsche Grammatik,** umfassend
die gothische, altnordische, altsächsische, angelsächsische
und althochdeutsche Sprache. Part I. 1 (Specielle Lautlehre). Leipzig, 1870. Part I. 2 (Vergleichung der
deutschen Laute untereinander) remained unfinished. Leipzig, 1875.

27

p **E. Wasserzieher.** Aus dem Leben der deutschen Sprache. Leipzig. No year. Very short and popular articles.

pc **August Schleicher.** Die deutsche Sprache. Stuttgart. ¹1860, ⁶1888 (very slight alterations).

Otto Behaghel. Geschichte der deutschen Sprache. (In Paul's Grundriss, I. 526-633.)

p **Otto Behaghel.** Die deutsche Sprache. (In : 'Das Wissen der Gegenwart,' LIV.) Leipzig, 1886. This book was translated (with some modifications) under the title : 'A short historical grammar of the German language,' by **Emil Trechmann.** London, 1891.

b **Albert J. W. Cerf.** Short Historical Grammar of the German Language. Old, Middle, and Modern High German. Part I. : Introduction and Phonology. London, 1894. Part II. containing the Accidence will follow soon.

b **Henri Lichtenberger.** Histoire de la langue allemande. Paris, 1895.

b **Friedrich Kauffmann.** Deutsche Grammatik. Marburg, 1888. (Short Gothic, O.H.G., M.H.G., N.H.G., phonology and accidence.)

a **Wilhelm Wilmanns.** Deutsche Grammatik. Strassburg. Vol. I. (Phonology), 1893. Three or four more parts to follow.

a **Friedrich Kluge.** Vorgeschichte der altgermanischen Dialekte. (In Paul's Grundriss, I. 300-406.)

a **Adolf Noreen.** Abriss der urgermanischen Lautlehre. Strassburg, 1894.

GERMAN LANGUAGE AND GRAMMAR

Otto Behaghel. Zur Frage nach einer mittelhochdeutschen Schriftsprache. Basel, 1886.

ac Heinrich Rückert. Geschichte der neuhochdeutschen Schriftsprache. Leipzig, 1875. 2 vols.

a Adolf Socin. Schriftsprache und Dialekte im Deutschen. Heilbronn, 1888.

Konrad Burdach. Die Einigung der neuhochdeutschen Schriftsprache. Halle, 1884. (Part of a hitherto unpublished greater work on the history of the German literary language.)

Friedrich Kluge. Von Luther bis Lessing. Strassburg, ¹1887, ²1888.

a Karl v. Bahder. Grundlagen des neuhochdeutschen Lautsystems. Strassburg, 1890.

H. Schultz. Die Bestrebungen der Sprachgesellschaften des 17. Jahrhunderts. Göttingen, 1888.

b Victor Henry. Précis de grammaire comparée de l'anglais et de l'allemand rapportés à leur commune origine et rapprochés des langues classiques. Paris, 1893. Translated by the author himself under the title: 'A short comparative grammar of English and German as traced back to their common origin and contrasted with the classical languages.' London, 1894.

K. G. Keller. Deutscher Antibarbarus. Beiträge zur Förderung des richtigen Gebrauchs der Muttersprache. Stuttgart, 1879, ²1886. (By G. Hauff.)

K. G. Andresen. Sprachgebrauch und Sprachrichtigkeit im Deutschen. Heilbronn, [1]1880. Leipzig, [7]1892.

Th. Matthias. Sprachleben und Sprachschäden. Leipzig, 1892.

[c] F. A. Brandstäter. Die Gallicismen in der deutschen Schriftsprache. Leipzig, 1874.

SYNOPSIS OF GRAMMATICAL FORMS.

Karl Müllenhoff. Paradigmata zur deutschen Grammatik. Zum Gebrauch für Vorlesungen. Sixth edition carefully revised by Max Roediger. Berlin, 1889. (Gothic, Old High German, Middle High German.)

Max Roediger. Paradigmata zur altsächsischen Grammatik im Anschluss an Müllenhoffs Paradigmata für seine Vorlesungen zusammengestellt. Berlin, 1883.

Oskar Schade. Paradigmen zur deutschen Grammatik. Gotisch, Althochdeutsch, Mittelhochdeutsch, Neu-hochdeutsch. Fourth edition. Halle, 1884.

Eduard Sievers. Paradigmen zur deutschen Grammatik. Gotisch, Altnordisch, Angelsächsisch, Altsächsisch, Althochdeutsch, Mittelhochdeutsch. Halle,[1]1874,[2]1876.

MODERN GERMAN GRAMMAR.

[b] Wilhelm Wilmanns. Deutsche Grammatik für die Unter- und Mittelklassen höherer Anstalten. Berlin, [8]1891.

ᵇ **Otto Lyon.** Handbuch der deutschen Sprache für höhere Schulen. Vol. I. Leipzig, ³1891.

J. Ch. A. Heyse. Deutsche Grammatik. New edition by Otto Lyon. Hannover, ²⁵1893. (Partly re-written.),

Theodor Gelbe. Deutsche Sprachlehre für höhere Lehranstalten sowie zum Selbststudium. Eisenach. No year. (Preface, 1877.) 2 vols.

ᵇ **Kuno Meyer.** A German Grammar for Schools. Based on the principles and requirements of the Grammatical Society. (Parallel Grammar Series.) London, I³. 1891 (Accidence), II¹. 1890 (Syntax).

A. L. Meissner. The Public School German Grammar. London, ¹1885, ⁵1893.

H. S. Beresford-Webb. A Practical German Grammar. London, ⁴1892.

C. E. Aue. Grammar of the German Language. London and Edinburgh, 1886.

H. W. Eve. A School German Grammar. London, ⁴1890.

Tr. H. Weisse. A complete Practical Grammar of the German Language, with exercises constituting a method and reader. London, ⁴1888.

W. D. Whitney. A Compendious German Grammar. London, 1880.

H. C. G. Brandt. A Grammar of the German Language for High Schools and Colleges. Designed for beginners and advanced students. Boston, U.S.A., ¹1884, ⁰1893.

WORD FORMATION.

[a] **Fr. Kluge.** Nominale Stammbildungslehre der alt-germanischen Dialekte. Halle, 1886.

[b] **Ad. Jeitteles.** Neuhochdeutsche Wortbildung. Auf Grundlage der historischen Grammatik für weitere Kreise bearbeitet. Wien, 1865.

[p] **J. Rey.** Die Wortbildung im Neuhochdeutschen. Eine Beispielsammlung für Schule und Haus. Aarau, 1893.

SYNTAX ALONE.

[a] **Theodor Vernaleken.** Deutsche Syntax. 2 vols. Wien, 1861 and 1863.

Oskar Erdmann. Grundzüge der deutschen Syntax. I. Stuttgart, 1886. (Not yet complete.)

Franz Kern. Die deutsche Satzlehre. Eine Untersuchung ihrer Grundlagen. Berlin, 1883, [2]1888.

Hermann Wunderlich. Der deutsche Satzbau. Stuttgart, 1892.

Hermann Wunderlich. Unsere Umgangssprache in der Eigenart ihrer Satzfügung dargestellt. Weimar and Berlin, 1894.

EARLY NEW HIGH GERMAN.

Raphael Meyer. Einführung in das ältere Neuhochdeutsche zum Studium der Germanistik. Leipzig, 1894. After the model of Zupitza's 'Einführung.' Cf. p. 44.

ac Joseph Kehrein. Grammatik der deutschen Sprache des funfzehnten bis siebenzehnten Jahrhunderts. I. (Phonology, Accidence) 1854. II. (Word-Formation), 1855. III. (Syntax) 1856, ²1863.

a Ältere deutsche Grammatiken in Neudrucken, herausgegeben von John Meier. Strassburg, 1894. Only No. II. published up till now.

a Joh. Müller. Quellenschriften und Geschichte des deutsch-sprachlichen Unterrichtes bis zur Mitte des 16. Jahrhunderts. Gotha, 1882.

SPECIAL MODERN AUTHORS.

E. Opitz. Ueber die Sprache Luthers. Halle, 1869.

Paul Pietsch. Martin Luther und die hochdeutsche Schriftsprache. Breslau, 1883.

Carl Franke. Grundzüge der Schriftsprache Luthers. Görlitz, 1888.

Hermann Wunderlich. Forschungen über den Satzbau Luthers. München, 1888.

Christoph Würfl. Ein Beitrag zur Kenntnis des Sprachgebrauchs Klopstocks. Gymnasialprogramme. Brünn, 1883-85.

F. Petri. Kritische Beiträge zur Geschichte der Dichtersprache Klopstocks. Dissertation. Greifswald, 1894.

c August Lehmann. Forschungen über Lessings Sprache. Braunschweig, 1875.

C

F. Thalmayr. Über Wielands Klassicität, Sprache
und Stil. Programm. Pilsen, 1894.

Theodor Längin. Die Sprache des jungen Herder in
ihrem Verhältnis zur Schriftsprache. Freiburger
Dissertation. Tauberbischofsheim, 1891.

ᶜ **August Lehmann.** Goethe's Sprache und ihr Geist.
Berlin, 1852.

Carl Olbrich. Goethes Sprache und die Antike. Leipzig,
1891.

Paul Knauth. Goethes Sprache und Stil im Alter.
Leipzig, 1894.

K. G. Andresen. Über die Sprache Jacob Grimms.
Leipzig, 1870.

MODERN GERMAN SPELLING.

**Verhandlungen der zur Herstellung grösserer Einigung
in der deutschen Rechtschreibung berufenen Kon-
ferenz.** Berlin, den 4 bis 15 Januar, 1876. Halle, 1876.]

**Regeln und Wörterverzeichnis für die deutsche Recht-
schreibung zum Gebrauch in den preussischen Schulen.**
(The official book.) Berlin, ²1887. Cf. Duden's Dictionary,
p. 51.

Wilhelm Wilmanns. Kommentar zur preussischen
Schulorthographie. Berlin, 1880. A new edition containing many alterations was published by Wilmanns in
1887 under the title 'Die Orthographie in den Schulen
Deutschlands.' Very valuable for teachers.

PUNCTUATION.

O. Glöde. Die deutsche Interpunktionslehre. Leipzig, 1893.

MODERN GERMAN PRONUNCIATION.

H. Huss. Die Lehre vom Accent der deutschen Sprache. Altenburg, 1877.

ᵇ **Wilhelm Vietor.** Die Aussprache des Schriftdeutschen. Mit dem 'Wörterverzeichnis für die deutsche Rechtschreibung zum Gebrauch in den preussischen Schulen' in phonetischer Umschrift sowie phonetischen Texten. Heilbronn, 1885. Leipzig, ³1895.

ᵇ **Wilhelm Vietor.** German Pronunciation. Practice and Theory. Heilbronn, 1885. Second improved edition, Leipzig, 1890.

ᵖ **Wilhelm Vietor.** Wie ist die Aussprache des Deutschen zu lehren? Ein Vortrag. Marburg, 1893.

ᵇ **Wilhelm Vietor.** Deutsche Lauttafel (System Vietor), nebst Erklärungen und Beispielen. (Text in German, English, and French.) Marburg, 1893. This table is more fully illustrated by the above-mentioned lecture.

Wilhelm Vietor. Elemente der Phonetik und Orthoepie des Deutschen, Englischen und Französischen, mit Rücksicht auf die Bedürfnisse der Lehrpraxis. Heilbronn, 1884, ²1887. Third improved edition, containing a very full bibliography, Leipzig, 1894.

GERMAN COMPOSITION.

ᵇ **A. L. Meissner.** Primer of German Composition. Short stories in easy English prose with explanatory notes, an English-German Vocabulary, and a list of strong and irregular verbs. London, 1894.

ᵇ **G. Eugène Fasnacht.** Macmillan's Course of German Composition. First Course. Parallel German-English extracts and parallel English-German syntax. London, 1890.

ᵇ **E. S. Buchheim.** Elementary German Prose Composition. Oxford, 1893.

C. A. Buchheim. Materials for German Prose Composition, or Selections from modern English Writers with grammatical notes, idiomatic renderings of difficult passages, a general introduction, and a grammatical index. London, ¹³1890. [Parts I. and II. were published separately under the title : **The First Book of German Prose Composition.** London, 1894.]

H. S. Beresford-Webb. Manual of German Composition, with passages for translation. London, ²1892.

Herm. Lange. German Composition. A theoretical and practical guide to the art of translating English prose into German. Oxford, ³1891.

Charles Harris. Selections for German Composition, with notes and vocabulary. Boston, U.S.A., 1890.

Horatio S. White. Selections for German Prose Composition, with notes and a complete vocabulary. Boston, U.S.A., 1891.

ESSAY WRITING.

(The following books were written to meet the wants of German schools. English teachers will have to adapt them to their purposes.)

ᵇ **K. A. Jul. Hoffmann.** Rhetorik für höhere Schulen. The later editions were edited by **Chr. Fr. A. Schuster.** Clausthal. 2 parts. I.⁶ (1883) ; II.⁵ (1882). Very useful.

ᵇ **L. W. Straub.** Aufsatzentwürfe. Stuttgart, ²1894. (Sammlung Göschen, N. 17.) Cheap and elementary.

ᵇ **Leo Cholevius.** Praktische Anleitung zur Abfassung deutscher Aufsätze, in Briefen an einen jungen Freund. Leipzig, ⁵1882.

Leo Cholevius. Dispositionen und Materialien zu deutschen Aufsätzen. Leipzig, 1860. The book has now appeared in the 8th edition.

Hermann Kluge. Themata zu deutschen Aufsätzen und Vorträgen. Für höhere Unterrichtsanstalten. Altenburg, 1876. The book has now appeared in the 6th edition.

Karl Menge. Ausführliche Dispositionen und Musterentwürfe zu deutschen Aufsätzen. Leipzig, 1890.

ᵃ **Ernst Laas.** Der deutsche Aufsatz in den oberen Gymnasialklassen. Theorie und Materialien. 2 parts. Third Edition, edited by **J. Imelmann.** Berlin, 1894.

Excellent for teachers, full of valuable material.

GERMAN HANDWRITING.

B. Lévy. Recueil de Lettres Allemandes reproduites en écritures autographiques pour exercer à la lecture des manuscrits allemands. Paris, [0]1892.

CONVERSATION.

[b] **Franz Lange.** Easy German Dialogues, specially compiled for the use of beginners and young pupils. London, 1893.

L. E. Wirth. German Chit-Chat, or Deutsche Plaudereien. London, [5]1888.

A. an der Halden. Progressive German Dialogues, with a synopsis of German construction, a collection of idioms indispensable for conversation, and notes. For schools and private study. London. New edition. 1893.

A. L. Meissner. Practical Lessons in German Conversation. London, 1888.

Albert Hamann. Echo of Spoken German, with a German-English vocabulary by **A. L. Becker.** Leipzig, 1892.

Excellent dialogues, useful introduction into the study of German life and manners.

TECHNICAL TERMS, NEWSPAPER GERMAN.

Francis Jones. A German Science Reader. London, 1892.

Harry Blake Hodges. A Course in Scientific German.
Boston, U.S.A., 1891.

F. Coverley Smith. Introduction to Commercial German. London, 1892.

H. Preisinger. A German Commercial Reader. London, 1893.

W. T. Jeffcott and G. J. Tossell. The German Newspaper Reading-Book. London, 1883.

PHRASES, IDIOMS, SLANG, POPULAR ETYMOLOGY, QUOTATIONS.

Albert Richter. Deutsche Redensarten. Sprachlich und kulturgeschichtlich erläutert. Leipzig, 1889.

Wilhelm Borchardt. Die sprichwörtlichen Redensarten im deutschen Volksmund nach Sinn und Ursprung erläutert. Leipzig, 1888 ; 2-41894. (By G. Wustmann.)

G. Wunderlich. Deutsche Redensarten. Second edition. Langensalza, 1886.

Hermann Schrader. Der Bilderschmuck der deutschen Sprache. Berlin, 11886, 21889.

Franz Söhns. Die Parias unserer Sprache. Eine Sammlung von Volksausdrücken. Heilbronn, 1888.

Arnold Genthe. Deutsches Slang. Eine Sammlung familiärer Ausdrücke und Redensarten. Strassburg, 1892.

Otto Kares. Poesie und Moral im Wortschatz. Essen, 1882.

Karl Gustav Andresen. Ueber deutsche Volksetymologie. ¹1876. ⁵Heilbronn, 1889.

Simon Widmann. Geschichtsel. Missverstandenes und Missverständliches aus der Geschichte gesammelt und erklärt. Paderborn, 1891. .

Georg Büchmann. Geflügelte Worte. Der Citatenschatz des deutschen Volkes, gesammelt und erläutert. Berlin, ¹1864. ¹⁰1889 (by **W. Robert-tornow**).

DIALECTS.

(Only some of the most important works can be enumerated.)

Karl Bernhardi. Sprachkarte von Deutschland. Kassel, 1844. Second improved edition (by **W. Stricker**), 1849.

ᶜ **Paul Piper.** Die Verbreitung der deutschen Dialekte bis um das Jahr 1300. Auf Grund der alten Sprachdenkmäler bearbeitet und kartographisch dargestellt. With a coloured map. Lahr, 1880.

Karl Weinhold. Über deutsche Dialektforschung. Die Laut- und Wortbildung und die Formen der schlesischen Mundart. Mit Rücksicht auf Verwandtes in den deutschen Dialekten. Ein Versuch. Wien, 1853.

Karl Weinhold. Grammatik der deutschen Mundarten. I. Alemannische Grammatik. Berlin, 1863. II. Bairische Grammatik. Berlin, 1867.

J. Winteler. Die Kerenzer Mundart des Kantons Glarus in ihren Grundzügen dargestellt. Leipzig, 1876.

Heinrich Rückert. Entwurf einer systematischen Darstellung der schlesischen Mundart im Mittelalter. Paderborn, 1878.

Karl Regel. Die Ruhlaer Mundart. Weimar, 1868.

Karl Nerger. Grammatik des meklenburgischen Dialektes älterer und neuerer Zeit. Laut- und Flexionslehre. Leipzig, 1869.

Friedrich Holthausen. Die Soester Mundart. Norden, 1886. (Ndd. Forschungen, I.)

Friedrich Kauffmann. Geschichte der schwäbischen Mundart im Mittelalter und in der Neuzeit. Mit Textproben und einer Geschichte der Schriftsprache in Schwaben. Strassburg, 1890.

For further information, cp. **Ferdinand Mentz.** Bibliographie der deutschen Mundartenforschung. Leipzig, 1892.

GRAMMAR OF SOME OF THE MOST IMPORTANT OLDER PERIODS AND AUTHORS.

(a) RUNIC INSCRIPTIONS.

Ludwig F. A. Wimmer. Die Runenschrift. Vom Verfasser überarbeitete und vermehrte Ausgabe. Aus dem Dänischen übersetzt von F. Holthausen. Berlin 1887. (The Danish original was published in 1874.)

[a] **Fritz Burg.** Die älteren nordischen Runeninschriften.
Berlin, 1885.

[a] **Rudolf Henning.** Die deutschen Runendenkmäler.
Strassburg, 1889.

Eduard Sievers. Runen und Runeninschriften (in Paul's
Grundriss I., 238-250, with a valuable table of Runic
alphabets.)

(*b*) Gothic.

[b] **Joseph Wright.** A Primer of the Gothic Language.
Oxford, 1892.

[b] **Wilhelm Braune.** Gotische Grammatik. Halle, [3]1887.
(The second edition of this book was translated into English
by C. H. Balg. New York, 1883.)

[ac] **H. C. v. d. Gabelentz** and **J. Loebe.** Ulfilas.
Leipzig, 1843-6. Additions in 1860. Vol. II., 2, 1846.

[ac] **Leo Meyer.** Die gothische Sprache. Berlin, 1869.

[b] **Moritz Heyne.** Ulfilas. Paderborn, [8]1885. (Grammar at
the end of the edition.)

Ernst Bernhardt. Kurzgefasste gotische Grammatik.
Halle, 1885.

T. le Marchant Douse. An Introduction, phonological,
morphological, syntactic, to the Gothic of Ulfilas.
London, 1886.

Eduard Sievers. Gotisch, in Paul's Grundriss, I. 407-16.

Karl Weinhold. Die gotische Sprache im Dienste des
Christenthums. Halle, 1870.

(c) OLD SAXON.

^c **J. H. Gallée.** Altsächsische Grammatik. I. (Phon-
ology and Inflexions). Halle, 1891. A second part containing the Old Saxon Syntax is being prepared by **Otto
Behaghel.** Compare also W. Braune's 'Abriss der althochdeutschen Grammatik,' mentioned below.

(d) MIDDLE LOW GERMAN.

^b **August Lübben.** Mittelniederdeutsche Grammatik
nebst Chrestomathie und Glossar. Leipzig, 1882.

(e) OLD HIGH GERMAN.

^b **Joseph Wright.** An Old High German Primer.
Oxford, 1888.

^b **Wilhelm Braune.** Abriss der althochdeutschen
Grammatik, nebst mittelhochdeutschen, altsächsischen und gotischen Paradigmen. Halle, 1891, ²1894.

Wilhelm Braune. Althochdeutsche Grammatik. Halle,
²1891.

^c **Paul Piper.** Litteraturgeschichte und Grammatik
des Althochdeutschen und Altsächsischen für Studirende bearbeitet. Paderborn, 1880.

The Grammar of important O.H.G. authors, e.g. Otfrid,
Tatian, etc., has been made the subject of special investigations.

a **Rudolf von Raumer.** Die Einwirkung des Christenthums auf die althochdeutsche Sprache. Stuttgart,
1845. (With an Appendix: Ein Wort der Verständigung
über die Schrift : Die Einwirkung, etc., by R. v. R.
Erlangen, 1852.)

a **Wilhelm Franz.** Die lateinisch-romanischen Elemente
im Althochdeutschen. Strassburg, 1884.

(*f*) MIDDLE HIGH GERMAN.

b **Julius Zupitza.** Einführung in das Studium des Mittelhochdeutschen. Zum Selbstunterricht für jeden
Gebildeten. Oppeln, ¹1868, ⁴1891.

b **Joseph Wright.** A Middle High German Primer.
Oxford, 1888.

b **Ernst Martin.** Mittelhochdeutsche Grammatik. Nebst
Wörterbuch zu der Nibelunge Nôt, zu den Gedichten
Walthers von der Vogelweide und zu Laurin. Für
den Schulgebrauch ausgearbeitet. Berlin, ⁸1878.

b **Hermann Paul.** Mittelhochdeutsche Grammatik.
Halle, ⁴1894. (Contains besides the phonology and accidence
a short sketch of M.H.G. Syntax.)

b **Oskar Brenner.** Mittelhochdeutsche Grammatik.
⁝ München, ²1890.

b **Karl Weinhold.** Kleine mittelhochdeutsche Grammatik. Wien, ²1889. (Phonology and accidence.)

Karl Weinhold. Mittelhochdeutsche Grammatik. Paderborn, ²1883. (Elaborate phonology and accidence.)

VI.

DICTIONARIES.

A.—OLD GERMAN DICTIONARIES FOR GENERAL USE.

Oskar Schade. Altdeutsches Wörterbuch. Halle, 1866 ²1872-82. 2 vols.

Wilhelm Wackernagel. Wörterbuch zum altdeutschen Lesebuch. Basel, ¹1861. Under the title 'Altdeutsches Handwörterbuch' it forms the fifth part of Wackernagel's 'Deutsches Lesebuch.' Basel, ⁵1878.

B.—DICTIONARIES FOR SPECIAL OLD GERMAN PERIODS AND AUTHORS.

(a) GOTHIC.

Ernst Schulze. Gothisches Glossar. Magdeburg, 1847. (Aims at absolute completeness.)

ᶜ **Ernst Schulze.** Gothisches Wörterbuch nebst Flexions- lehre. Züllichau, 1867. (The etymologies are unsatis- factory.)

ᵃᶜ **Lorenz Diefenbach.** Vergleichendes Wörterbuch der gothischen Sprache. Frankfurt-a-M., 1851. Two vols.

Sigmund Feist. Grundriss der gotischen Etymologie. Strassburg, 1888.

45

^c **G. H. Balg.** A Comparative Glossary of the Gothic Language, with especial reference to English and German. Mayville, 1887-89.

Oskar Priese. Deutsch-Gotisches Wörterbuch. Leipzig, 1890.

(*b*) OLD SAXON.

J. Andreas Schmeller. Glossarium Saxonicum. München, 1840. (Part II. of his edition of Heliand.)

Moritz Heyne. Heliand. Mit ausführlichem Glossar herausgegeben. Paderborn, ³1883. (Very useful glossary. The O.H.G. and Old English equivalents are given in brackets.)

(*c*) MIDDLE LOW GERMAN.

Karl Schiller and **August Lübben.** Mittelniederdeutsches Wörterbuch. Five volumes and a Supplement. Bremen, 1875-81.

August Lübben and **Christoph Walther.** Mittelniederdeutsches Handwörterbuch. Norden und Leipzig, 1888. One volume. Finished by Walther after Lübben's death. (Wörterbücher des Vereins für niederdeutsche Sprachforschung. Vol. III. Abbrev. :—**Ndd. Wbb.** Bd. 3.)

(*d*) OLD HIGH GERMAN.

^{ac} **E. G. Graff.** Althochdeutscher Sprachschatz oder Wörterbuch der althochdeutschen Sprache. Berlin, 1834-42. Six volumes. A seventh part, being a complete alphabetical index to Graff's Dictionary, in which the words were arranged according to roots, was published by H. F. Massmann under a separate title.

^c **H. F. Massmann.** Gedrängtes althochdeutsches Wörterbuch oder vollständiger alphabetischer Index zu dem althochdeutschen Sprachschatz von E. G. Graff. Berlin, 1864.

The O.H.G. vocabulary has, to a very great extent, been worked into the two more recent Old German Dictionaries by **W. Wackernagel** and by **O. Schade.** (*See* Old German Dictionaries, page 44.)

The vocabulary of Otfrid has been treated specially in the works of **J. Kelle** and of **P. Piper.** Cf. pp. 85, 86.

(*e*) MIDDLE HIGH GERMAN.

^a **Benecke-Müller-Zarncke.** Mittelhochdeutsches Wörterbuch mit Benutzung des Nachlasses von J. Benecke ausgearbeitet von **W. Müller** und **F. Zarncke.** Leipzig 1854-68. Four volumes. (The words are not arranged alphabetically, but according to stems.)
[Abbrev. :—**Mhd. Wb.**]

Matthias Lexer. Mittelhochdeutsches Handwörterbuch. Zugleich als Supplement und alphabetischer Index zum mittelhochdeutschen Wörterbuch von Benecke-Müller-Zarncke. Leipzig, 1872-78. Three vols.
[Abbrev. :—**Mhd. Hwb.**]

These seven volumes together form the great **MHD. WB.**, in works on MHG. often simply called **WB.**

Matthias Lexer. Mittelhochdeutsches Taschenwörterbuch. Leipzig, ¹1879, ⁴1892.
[Abbrev. :—**Mhd. Twb.**]

SPECIAL M.H.G. GLOSSARIES.

C. August Hornig. Glossarium zu den Gedichten Walther's von der Vogelweide nebst einem Reimverzeichniss. Quedlinburg, 1844.

F. Benecke. Wörterbuch zu Hartmanns Iwein. Göttingen, 1833, ²1874 (edited by **E. Wilken**).

A. Lübben. Wörterbuch zu der Nibelunge Nôt. Oldenburg, ¹1854, ³1877.

K. Bartsch. Der Nibelunge Nôt. Large edition. II. 2 (Glossary). Leipzig, 1880.

C.—NEW HIGH GERMAN DICTIONARIES.

(*a*) GENERAL WORKS.

Jacob Grimm and **Wilhelm Grimm.** Deutsches Wörterbuch. Leipzig. Since 1854. Continued after the death of the brothers Grimm by **K. Weigand, M. Lexer,** and **R. Hildebrand,** who are now deceased, and **M. Heyne, E. Wülcker, K. Kant, Oskar Erdmann.** Not yet completed. Finished are : **A—Gesetz, H—Schleier, T— Todestag, V—Verpetschieren.** The work will be completed in 12 volumes, of which 8 are now ready.

[Abbrev. :—**DW.**, *or* **DWb.**, *or* **DWB.**]

Daniel Sanders. Wörterbuch der deutschen Sprache. Mit Belegen von Luther bis auf die Gegenwart. 3 Vols. Leipzig, 1860-65.

Daniel Sanders. Ergänzungs-Wörterbuch der deutschen Sprache. Berlin, 1885. This is a very full supplement to the preceding work.

Daniel Sanders. Handwörterbuch der deutschen Sprache. Leipzig, ²1878.

ᶜ Fr. L. Karl Weigand. Deutsches Wörterbuch. 2 vols. Giessen, ⁴1881-82. Some of the etymologies of this excellent work are now superseded.

Moritz Heyne. Deutsches Wörterbuch. Since 1890. Leipzig. Will be complete in 3 vols. Two vols. and the first half of the third have been published. The last part will follow in 1895. Enumeration of the principal older dictionaries in Vol. II., pp. xxii-xxiii. Most useful.

Lorenz Diefenbach and Ernst Wülcker. Hoch- und niederdeutsches Wörterbuch der mittleren und neueren Zeit. Zur Ergänzung der vorhandenen Wörterbücher, insbesondere des der Gebrüder Grimm. Frankfurt am Main, 1874.

Daniel Sanders. Deutscher Sprachschatz, geordnet nach Begriffen zur leichten Auffindung und Auswahl des passenden Ausdrucks. Ein stilistisches Hülfsbuch für jeden Deutsch Schreibenden. 2 vols. Hamburg, 1873-77. (Similar to Roget's 'Thesaurus of English Words and Phrases.')

(b) SPECIAL AUTHORS.

Philipp Dietz. Wörterbuch zu Dr. Martin Luthers deutschen Schriften. Leipzig. Vol. I. (A-F). 1870. Vol. II., 1 (G-Hals). 1872. Valuable. Not continued.

(c) ETYMOLOGY.

Friedrich Kluge. Etymologisches Wörterbuch der deutschen Sprache. Strassburg, ¹1882, ⁵1894. Enumera-
D

tion of the principal older dictionaries, xxv-xxvi. There is
an English translation from the fourth German edition by
J. F. Davis. London, 1891. Very full indices to this
book were compiled by **V. F. Janssen.**

Vincent Franz Janssen. Gesamtindex zu Kluges ety-
mologischem Wörterbuch der deutschen Sprache.
Strassburg, 1890.

ᵖ **Konrad Duden.** Etymologie der neuhochdeutschen
Sprache. München, 1893.

(*d*) SYNONYMS.

J. A. Eberhard. Synonymisches Handwörterbuch der
deutschen Sprache. Halle, 1802. 14th edition (thoroughly
revised and augmented by **Otto Lyon**). Leipzig, 1889.

ᵃ **F. L. Karl Weigand.** Wörterbuch der deutschen
Synonymen. 3 vols. Mainz, 1840-43, ²1852.

Daniel Sanders. Wörterbuch der deutschen Synonymen.
Hamburg, 1872, ²1882.

(*e*) FOREIGN WORDS.

J. Ch. A. Heyse. Allgemeines Fremdwörterbuch. Nordhausen, 1807. Berlin, ¹⁶1879.

Daniel Sanders. Fremdwörterbuch. 2 vols. Leipzig,
1871 ²1891-92.

Richard Förtsch. Die Fremdwörter der deutschen
Sprache, ihre Erklärung, Verdeutschung, Aussprache,
etc. Braunschweig, 1889.

(*f*) German Equivalents of Foreign Words.

Hermann Dunger. Wörterbuch von Verdeutschungen entbehrlicher Fremdwörter. Leipzig, 1882.

Daniel Sanders. Verdeutschungswörterbuch. Leipzig, 1884.

Otto Sarrazin. Verdeutschungswörterbuch. Berlin, [2]1889.

(*g*) Spelling.

Konrad Duden. Vollständiges orthographisches Wörterbuch der deutschen Sprache, mit etymologischen Angaben, kurzen Sacherklärungen und Verdeutschungen der Fremdwörter. Nach den neuen amtlichen Regeln. Leipzig and Wien, [4]1894.

(*h*) Grammar and Style.

[p] **Daniel Sanders.** Wörterbuch der Hauptschwierigkeiten in der deutschen Sprache. Grosse Ausgabe. Berlin, [10]1889.

[p] **J. E. Wessely.** Grammatisch-stilistisches Wörterbuch der deutschen Sprache. Leipzig, 1883.

(*i*) Dialects.

(*Only some of the most notable books are here enumerated.*)

J. Andreas [Schmeller. Bayerisches Wörterbuch. 2d ed. by **K. Frommann.** München, [1]1827-1837, [2]1872-77.

J. Cp. v. Schmid. Schwäbisches Wörterbuch, mit etymologischen und historischen Anmerkungen. Stuttgart, 1831, [2]1844.

Matthias Lexer. Kärntisches Wörterbuch. Leipzig 1862.

Schweizerisches Idiotikon. Wörterbuch der schweizerdeutschen Sprache, edited by **Friedrich Staub** and **Ludwig Tobler,** and others. Frauenfeld. Since 1881. In progress.

A. F. C. Vilmar. Idiotikon von Kurhessen. Marburg, 1868, ²1883. 'Nachträge' to this work were published by **H. v. Pfister.** Marburg, 1886.

Versuch eines bremisch-niedersächsischen Wörterbuchs, edited by the **Bremische deutsche Gesellschaft.** Parts 1-5. Bremen, 1767-71. Part 6. Bremen, 1869. The last part (6) was reprinted in 1881.

J. F. Schütze. Holsteinisches Idiotikon. Parts 1-3. Hamburg, 1800-1802. Part 4. Altona, 1806.

Georg Schambach. Wörterbuch der niederdeutschen Mundart der Fürstenthümer Göttingen und Grubenhagen. Hannover, 1858.

J. F. Danneil. Wörterbuch der altmärkisch-plattdeutschen Mundart. Salzwedel, 1859.

J. ten Doornkaat Koolman. Wörterbuch der ostfriesischen Sprache. 3 vols. Norden, 1879-85.

Fr. Woeste. Wörterbuch der westfälischen Mundart. Norden and Leipzig, 1882. (Niederdeutsche Wörterbücher, Vol. I.)

(*k*) ENGLISH-GERMAN AND GERMAN-ENGLISH DICTIONARIES.

(Only a very few of the great number can be enumerated here.)

ᵖ **Richard Jäschke.** English-German Conversation Dictionary. London, 1893. Handy and useful for persons travelling in Germany.

ᵇ **Martin Krummacher.** A Dictionary of every-day German and English. 2 parts in 1 volume. London, no year (1892).

ᵇ **William Dwight Whitney.** A compendious German and English Dictionary. 2 parts in 1 volume. London, 1884.

ᵇ **Elizabeth Weir.** Cassell's New German Dictionary. 2 parts in 1 volume. London, ¹1888, ²1892.

ᵇ **Friedrich Koehler.** Dictionary of the English and German Languages. Entirely remodelled and greatly enlarged, by **Hermann Lambeck.** 2 Parts in 1 volume. Leipzig, ³⁰1892.

Gustav Krüger. Systematical English-German Vocabulary. Englisch-Deutsches Wörterbuch nach Stoffen geordnet. Für Studierende, Schulen und Selbstunterricht. Berlin, 1893.

Newton Ivory Lucas. Englisch-Deutsches und Deutsch-Englisches Wörterbuch. 4 vols. Bremen, 1854-68.

Felix Flügel. Allgemeines Englisch-Deutsches und Deutsch-Englisches Wörterbuch. Fourth entirely remodelled edition. 2 parts in 3 volumes. Braunschweig, 1891. An abridged edition of this work in two volumes is in course of preparation.

Ed. Muret. Encyklopädisches Englisch-Deutsches und Deutsch-Englisches Wörterbuch. In progress. Since 1891. Berlin.

This work will consist of four large volumes, the first of which (English-German, Part I.) is now (1894) complete.

Gustav Eger. Technologisches Wörterbuch in englischer und deutscher Sprache. With the assistance of many experts, and technically revised and enlarged by **Otto Brandes.** 2 volumes. Braunschweig, 1882-84.

E. Röhrig. Technologisches Wörterbuch. Deutsch-Englisch-Französisch. Wiesbaden, ³1887.

F. J. Wershoven. Technical Vocabulary. English-German. For Scientific, Technical and Industrial Students. London, 1885.

Charles Scholl. Phraseological Dictionary of Commercial Correspondence. English-German. Assisted by **G. Macaulay.** London, 1886.

VII.

NAMES.

ᴬᶜ **A. F. Pott.** Die Personen-Namen, insbesondere die Familiennamen und ihre Entstehungsarten; auch unter Berücksichtigung der Ortsnamen. Eine sprachliche Untersuchung. Leipzig, 1853, ²1859.

August Fick. Die griechischen Personen-Namen nach ihrer Bildung erklärt, mit den Namensystemen verwandter Sprachen verglichen und systematisch geordnet. Göttingen, 1874.

H. F. Otto Abel. Die deutschen Personen-Namen. Berlin, 1853; ²1889. (Ed. **Walter Robert-tornow.**)

ᴾ **Ferdinand Khull.** Deutsches Namenbüchlein. Ein Hausbuch zur Mehrung des Verständnisses unserer heimischen Vornamen und zur Förderung deutscher Namengebung. This is one of the publications of the 'Allgemeiner deutscher Sprachverein.' Braunschweig, 1891.

R. Kapff. Deutsche Vornamen mit den von ihnen abstammenden Geschlechtsnamen sprachlich erläutert. Nürtingen am Neckar, 1889.

Ludwig Steub. Die oberdeutschen Familien-Namen. München, 1870.

[p] **A. F. C. Vilmar.** Deutsches Namenbüchlein. Die Entstehung und Bedeutung der deutschen Familiennamen. Marburg, 1865, [5]1880.

Albert Heintze. Die deutschen Familien-Namen geschichtlich, geographisch, sprachlich. Halle, 1882.

Wilhelm Deecke. Die deutschen Verwandtschaftsnamen. Weimar, 1870.

Paul Feit. De Germanorum nominibus propriis compositis. Osterprogramm. Lübeck, 1875.

Friedrich Stark. Die Kosenamen der Germanen. Wien, 1868. The articles were originally published in the WSB. of 1866.

K. G. Andresen. Konkurrenzen in der Erklärung der deutschen Geschlechtsnamen. Heilbronn, 1883.

[ac] **Ernst Förstemann.** Altdeutsches Namenbuch. I. Personen-Namen. Nordhausen, 1854. II. Ortsnamen. 1856-9, [2]1872. A valuable collection of names occurring in documents earlier than 1200.

Ernst Förstemann. Die deutschen Ortsnamen. Nordhausen, 1863.

R. Rösler. Über die Namen der Wochentage. Wien, 1865.

Karl Weinhold. Die deutschen Monatnamen. Halle, 1869.

More information is given in K. v. Bahder's 'Grundriss,' pp. 143 sqq., and in the 'Jahresberichte' published by the 'Berliner Gesellschaft für deutsche Philologie.' Cf. p. 19.

VIII.

LITERATURE.

A.—GENERAL WORKS.

[a] **August Koberstein.** Grundriss der Geschichte der deutschen Nationallitteratur. Leipzig, 1827. 5th ed. complete in five vols., Leipzig, 1872-4 (this edition was brought out after Koberstein's death by **K. Bartsch**). Of the 6th revised edition only the first volume (from the earliest times to the end of the 16th century) was brought out by Bartsch. Leipzig, 1884. No more has been published.

[a] **Karl Goedeke.** Grundrisz zur Geschichte der deutschen Dichtung. Aus den Quellen. Hannover (-Dresden), [1]I (1859)—III. (1881). The second edition has been entirely rewritten, vols. I.—III. (1884-1887) by Goedeke himself, the following volumes after the author's death by various eminent specialists under the editorship of **Edmund Goetze**. Vol. IV. (1891): the great classics of the 18th century up to Schiller ; and Vol. V., including Schiller's life, are now complete. For the time after Schiller's death the third volume of the first edition contains much valuable material. A most valuable bibliography, indispensable for every scholar.

[a] **Wilhelm Wackernagel.** Geschichte der deutschen Litteratur. Ein Handbuch. Basel, 1848-55. The second edition was edited and partly (17th-19th centuries) written by **Ernst Martin.** Vol. I. Basel, 1879 (from the earliest

times to the end of the 15th century). Vol. II. (from the
16th century to the present time). Basel, 1885-1894. The
work contains many valuable biographical references.

^a **Georg G. Gervinus.** Geschichte der deutschen Dich-
tung. Leipzig, 1835. The 5th ed. in five volumes (partly
edited by **K. Bartsch**). Leipzig, 1871-74.

^p **Heinrich Kurz.** Geschichte der deutschen Litteratur
mit ausgewählten Stücken aus den Werken der vorzüglichsten Schriftsteller. Mit vielen nach den besten
Originalen und Zeichnungen ausgeführten Illustra-
tionen in Holzschnitt. Leipzig, 1851-59. Last complete
edition in four vols. ⁸I. ⁸II. ⁷III. ⁴IV. ; Leipzig, 1892.

Wilhelm Scherer. Geschichte der deutschen Litteratur.
Berlin, 1882-5, ⁷1894. Contains a very usefully selected
bibliography. [English translation in two volumes by **Mrs.
Conybeare**; Oxford, 1885. Part of it : ' A History of
German Literature from the accession of Frederick the
Great to the death of Goethe.' Oxford, 1891.]

^p **Otto Roquette.** Geschichte der deutschen Dichtung,
von den ältesten Denkmälern bis auf die Neuzeit.
Frankfurt am Main, 1866, ³1882.

^p **Robert Koenig.** Deutsche Litteraturgeschichte.
Bielefeld und Leipzig, 1878, ²³1893. 2 vols. Contains many
interesting illustrations.

Jakob Baechtold. Geschichte der deutschen Litteratur
in der Schweiz. Frauenfeld, 1887-92. With useful biographical notes and learned discussions at the end of the
volume.

Leo Cholevius. Geschichte der deutschen Poesie nach ihren antiken Elementen. 2 vols. Leipzig, 1854-56.

J. Imelmann. Deutsche Dichtung im Liede. Gedichte litteraturgeschichtlichen Inhalts gesammelt und mit Anmerkungen begleitet. Berlin, 1880.

Friedrich Kirchner. Synchronismus zur deutschen National-Litteratur. Von der frühesten Zeit bis 1884. Berlin, 1885.

Gustav Koennecke. Bilderatlas zur Geschichte der deutschen Nationallitteratur. Ergänzung zu jeder deutschen Litteraturgeschichte. Enthaltend 1675 Abbildungen. Nach den Quellen. Marburg, 1887. A new edition is in course of publication (since 1894).

B.—SPECIAL PERIODS.

(a.) OLD GERMAN LITERATURE.

ᵃAdolf Ebert. Allgemeine Geschichte der Litteratur. des Mittelalters im Abendlande. Vol. III.: Die nationalen Litteraturen von ihren Anfängen und die lateinische Litteratur vom Tode Karls des Kahlen bis zum Beginne des elften Jahrhunderts. Leipzig, 1887.

ᵃJohann Kelle. Geschichte der deutschen Litteratur von der ältesten Zeit bis zur Mitte des elften Jahrhunderts. Berlin, 1892.

ᵃ Rudolf Koegel. Althoch- und Altniederdeutsche Litteratur. In Paul's Grundriss, Vol. II., 159-244. A special and much larger work on Old German Literature is being prepared by Koegel, under the title:

ᵃ **Rudolf Koegel.** Geschichte der deutschen Litteratur
bis zum Ausgange des Mittelalters. Strassburg, 1894.
Vol. I., 1 has been published. Will be complete in two
volumes.

Wolfgang Golther. Geschichte der deutschen Litteratur von den ersten Anfängen bis zum Ausgang des
Mittelalters. Stuttgart. No year (1892). This is vol.
163, 1 of Kürschner's Deutsche Nationallitteratur.

ᵃᶜ **Paul Piper.** Litteraturgeschichte und Grammatik des
Althochdeutschen und Altsächsischen für Studirende
bearbeitet. Paderborn, 1880.

ᵖᶜ **Paul Piper.** Die älteste deutsche Litteratur bis um das
Jahr 1050. Berlin and Stuttgart. No year (1885). This
is Vol. I. of Kürschner's Deutsche Nationallitteratur.

ᵃᶜ **Wilhelm Scherer.** Geschichte der deutschen Dichtung im elften und zwölften Jahrhundert. Strassburg,
1875. (QF. XII.)

Friedrich Vogt. Mittelhochdeutsche Literatur. In
Paul's Grundriss, II. 245-418.

ᶜ **Hermann Jellinghaus.** Mittelniederdeutsche Literatur. In Paul's Grundriss, II. 419-452.

ᵖ **Ferdinand Khull.** Geschichte der altdeutschen Dichtung. Graz, 1886. Aims at being a supplement to
Scherer's History of Literature.

ᵃᶜ **Ludwig Uhland.** Geschichte der altdeutschen Poesie.
Vorlesungen an der Universität Tübingen gehalten in
den Jahren 1830 und 1831. Edited after his death by
A. v. Keller and L. Holland; Stuttgart, 1865-6; in the col-

lected scientific works of the poet, under the title : Schriften
zur Geschichte der Dichtung und Sage. Vols. I. and II.
Cf. p. 16.

The best treatment of the Literature of the **sixteenth
century** is given by **Karl Goedeke** in the new edition of
the Grundriss. Vol. II. Dresden, 1886.

^a **Charles H. Herford.** Studies in the literary relations
of England and Germany in the sixteenth century.
Cambridge, 1886.

(β.) MODERN GERMAN LITERATURE.

Karl Borinski. Die Poetik der Renaissance und die
Anfänge der litterarischen Kritik in Deutschland.
Berlin, 1886.

^a **Julian Schmidt.** Geschichte des geistigen Lebens in
Deutschland von Leibniz bis auf Lessings Tod.
(1681-1781.) 2 Vols. Leipzig, 1862 and 1864.

^a **Julian Schmidt.** Geschichte der deutschen Litteratur
seit Lessings Tod. (1781-1867). 3 Vols. 5th edition.
Leipzig, 1866-7.

These two works have been recently united by the author
into one great history of modern German thought and
literature, under the title :

^a **Geschichte der deutschen Litteratur von Leibniz
bis auf unsere Zeit.** Vol. I. (1670-1763) ; II. (1763-
81) ; III. (1781-97) ; IV. (1797-1814). Berlin, 1886-90.
The fifth volume which was to complete the work was not
published.

Karl Lemcke. Geschichte der deutschen Dichtung neuerer Zeit. Vol. I. (From Opitz to Klopstock.)

ᵃ **Joseph Hillebrand.** Die deutsche Nationalliteratur im 18. und 19. Jahrhundert, historisch und aesthetisch-kritisch dargestellt. Third edition. 3 Vols. (By **Karl Hillebrand.**) Gotha, 1875.

ᵃ **Hermann Hettner.** Geschichte der deutschen Litteratur im achtzehnten Jahrhundert. [This is the third part of Hettner's 'Litteraturgeschichte des achtzehnten Jahrhunderts.' Part I.: England (5th edition, 1894, by Aloys Brandl). Part II.: France (5th edition, by H. Morf). Part III.: Germany.] The History of German Literature consists of three subdivisions and makes two volumes. The 4th improved edition will be completed before long. Braunschweig, 1893-5 (by **Otto Harnack**). A very useful index to this work was compiled by **Rudolf Grosse.** Braunschweig, 1883.

Hermann Hettner. Die romantische Schule in ihrem inneren Zusammenhange mit Goethe und Schiller. Braunschweig, 1850.

ᵃ **Rudolf Haym.** Die romantische Schule. Ein Beitrag zur Geschichte des deutschen Geistes. Berlin, 1870.

Paul Nerrlich. Jean Paul und seine Zeitgenossen. Berlin, 1876.

ᵇ **Johann Wilhelm Schaefer.** Geschichte der deutschen Litteratur des achtzehnten Jahrhunderts in übersichtlichen Umrissen und biographischen Schilderungen. In one volume or in 10 parts. Second edition, entirely re-written by **Franz Muncker.** Leipzig. No year.

P **Karl Borinski.** Geschichte der deutschen Litteratur seit dem Ausgang des Mittelalters. Stuttgart. No year (1894). This is Vol. 163, 2 of Kürschner's DNL.

Rudolf v. Gottschall. Die deutsche Nationallitteratur des neunzehnten Jahrhunderts. Litterarhistorisch und kritisch dargestellt. Breslau, 1854. 6th enlarged edition, 4 vols. Breslau, 1892.

c **H. Brandes.** Die Litteratur des 19. Jahrhunderts in ihren Hauptströmungen dargestellt. Vol. II. (Die romantische Schule in Deutschland). Leipzig, 1887. Vol. VI. (Das junge Deutschland). Leipzig, 1891.

C.—PRIMERS.

James K. Hosmer. A Short History of German Literature. Revised Edition. London, 1892. Based on the work of **H. Kurz.**

Hermann Kluge. Geschichte der deutschen National-Litteratur. Altenburg, 1869, ²⁵1894. (Adapted for English students by **Isabel T. Lublin,** under the title 'Primer of German Literature.' London, 1888. The short bibliographical notes of the German original are omitted in the English translation, which is not free from inaccuracies.)

Gottlob Egelhaaf. Grundzüge der deutschen Litteraturgeschichte. Heilbronn, 1881 ; Leipzig, ¹⁰1894.

Otto Lyon. Litteraturgeschichte, in his **Handbuch der deutschen Sprache für höhere Schulen II.** (Stilistik, Poetik, Litteraturgeschichte). Leipzig, 1885, ³1893. Contains short bibliographical notes. The History of Literature may be bought separately.

Max Koch. Geschichte der deutschen Litteratur.
Stuttgart, 1893. [Sammlung Goeschen, No. 31.]

G. Bötticher and **K. Kinzel.** Geschichte der deutschen
Litteratur. Halle, 1894.
[Anhang zu den Denkmälern der älteren deutschen
Litteratur, p. 80.]

D.—GENERAL BIOGRAPHY.

Allgemeine Deutsche Biographie, herausgegeben
durch die historische Commission bei der königl.
(bairischen) **Akademie der Wissenschaften.** Leipzig.
Since 1875. (Abbrev. :—**ADB.**)

Thirty-six volumes are now completed. Vol. XXXVII.
(-Thiemo) is still unfinished. All living men are excluded.
'German' is taken in the widest sense of the word ; *e.g.* Old
Netherlanders, if important for Germany, are noticed.

Franz Brümmer. Lexikon der deutschen Dichter und
Prosaisten von den ältesten Zeiten bis zum Ende des
18. Jahrhunderts. Leipzig. Reclams Universalbibliothek.

Franz Brümmer. Lexikon der deutschen Dichter und
Prosaisten des neunzehnten Jahrhunderts. 2 Parts in
1 Vol. Leipzig. Reclams Universalbibliothek.

Franz Bornmüller. Biographisches Schriftsteller-Lexi-
kon der Gegenwart. Die bekanntesten Zeitgenossen
auf dem Gebiet der Nationallitteratur aller Völker
mit Angabe ihrer Werke. Leipzig, 1882.

Joseph Kürschner. Deutscher Litteratur-Kalender auf das Jahr 1894. Sechzehnter Jahrgang. Stuttgart.
This annual contains the most reliable information about all living German authors.

E.—BIOGRAPHIES OF CLASSICAL WRITERS.

Only some of the most important biographies of the Classics can be enumerated here. For more information, cp. Goedeke's Grundriss and the ADB. Some important biographies are contained in or planned for Bettelheim's Series, *Führende Geister*, now called *Geisteshelden*. Dresden. Some short biographies in English are contained in the 'Great Writers' Series (Goethe by Sime, Schiller by Nevinson, Lessing by Rolleston).

Walther von der Vogelweide :

c **Ludwig Uhland.** W. v. d. Vogelweide, ein alt- • deutscher Dichter. Stuttgart, 1822.

Wilhelm Wilmanns. Leben und Dichten Walthers v. d. Vogelweide. Bonn, 1882.

p **Anton Schönbach.** Walther v. d. Vogelweide. Ein Dichterleben. Dresden, 1890.

Luther :

Julius Köstlin. Martin Luther. Sein Leben und seine Schriften. 4th edition. 2 vols. Berlin, 1888.

p **Julius Köstlin.** Luthers Leben. Leipzig, 1882, ⁹1891. With numerous authentic illustrations.
There is an anonymous translation of his work : 'Life of Luther.' London, 1883.

E

Hans Sachs :

P **Edmund Götze.** **Hans Sachs.** Bamberg, 1890.
(Bayerische Bibliothek, vol. 19.)

P **Rudolf Genée.** **Hans Sachs und seine Zeit.**
Berlin, 1894.

Ch. Schweitzer. Étude sur la vie et les œuvres de
Hans Sachs. Paris, 1887.

Klopstock :

Franz Muncker. **F. G. Klopstock. Geschichte
seines Lebens und seiner Schriften.** Stuttgart, 1888.

Wieland :

No first-rate work on him has been published as yet.
Cp. Goedeke's Grundriss, ²IV. § 223. A biography is being
prepared by B. Seuffert.

Lessing :

Th. W. Danzel and **G. E. Guhrauer. G. E. Lessing.
Sein Leben und seine Werke.** 1850-54. Zweite
berichtigte und vermehrte Aufl. herausgg. v. W.
v. Maltzahn und R. Boxberger. Berlin, 1880-1881.
2 volumes.

**Erich Schmidt. Lessing. Geschichte seines Lebens
und seiner Schriften.** 2 volumes. Berlin, 1884-92.

Herder :

ª **Rudolf Haym. Herder nach seinem Leben und
seinen Werken.** 2 vols. Berlin, 1877-85.

Eugen Kühnemann. Herders Leben. München,
1895.

Goethe :

Herman Grimm. Goethe. University Lectures. Berlin, 1876, ⁶1894. (English translation by **Miss S. Holland Adams** : 'The Life and Times of Goethe.' Boston, U.S.A., ¹1879, ²1881.)

Johann Wilhelm Schaefer. Goethe's Leben. 2 vols. Leipzig, 1877.

Richard M. Meyer. Goethe. Berlin, 1894. 3 Parts in 1 Volume.

This work forms parts 13-15 of the Series 'Geisteshelden' (originally 'Führende Geister'), eine Sammlung von Biographien, edited by A. Bettelheim.

ᶜ **George H. Lewes.** The Life and Works of Goethe, with sketches of his age and contemporaries from published and unpublished sources. 2 volumes. London, 1855, ³1875. (An abridgment of this work was published under the title : 'The story of Goethe's life.' London, 1873.)

Wilhelm Scherer. Aufsätze über Goethe. Berlin, 1886.

Woldemar v. Biedermann. Goethe-Forschungen. 2 volumes. Frankfurt am Main, I. (1879), II. (1886).

Victor Hehn. Gedanken über Goethe. ²Berlin, 1888.

John R. Seeley. Goethe reviewed after sixty years. London, 1894. Part of the essays contained in this book were published in the *Contemporary Review* of 1884.

Schiller :

[ac] **Karl Hoffmeister.** Schiller's Leben, Geistesent-
wickelung und Werke im Zusammenhang. Stuttgart. Five parts in 3 volumes. 1838-42.

[pc] **Karl Hoffmeister** and **Heinrich Viehoff.** Schiller's Leben für den weiteren Kreis seiner Leser.
Three parts. Second edition. Stuttgart, 1854. Abridgment of the above-mentioned work.

Some new Lives of Schiller are now in course of publication, viz. :

[p] **Otto Brahm.** Schiller. Will be complete in 2 vols.
Berlin, I. (1888), II., 1 (1892).

[a] **Richard Weltrich.** Friedrich Schiller. Geschichte
seines Lebens und Charakteristik seiner Werke.
Unter kritischem Nachweis der biographischen
Quellen. Part I. (1885), II. (1889). Stuttgart. Ex-
haustive. Will take a long time to be completed.

[a] **Jakob Minor.** Schiller. Sein Leben und seine
Werke. Berlin, I. (1890), II. (1890). Will be completed in about three more volumes. Most useful.

Jean Paul :

Paul Nerrlich. Jean Paul. Berlin, 1890.

Uhland :

Friedrich Notter. Ludwig Uhland. Sein Leben
und seine Dichtungen. Stuttgart, 1863.

Hermann Fischer. Ludwig Uhland. Eine Studie.
Stuttgart, 1887.

Kleist :

Otto Brahm. Heinrich von Kleist. Berlin, 1884. ³1892.

F.—HISTORY OF THE GERMAN NOVEL.

Wilhelm Scherer. Die Anfänge des deutschen Prosa-romans und Jörg Wickram von Colmar. Eine Kritik. (Criticism of the first part of Bobertag's 'Geschichte des Romans.') QF. xxi. Strassburg, 1877.

Leo Cholevius. Die bedeutendsten deutschen Romane des 17. Jahrhunderts. Leipzig, 1866.

Erich Schmidt. Richardson, Rousseau und Goethe. Ein Beitrag zur Geschichte des Romans im 18. Jahrhundert. Jena, 1875.

Jos. v. Eichendorff. Der deutsche Roman des 18. Jahr-hunderts in seinem Verhältniss zum Christenthum. Paderborn, 1866.

Fr. Kreyssig. Vorlesungen über den deutschen Roman der Gegenwart. Literar- und culturhistorische Studien. Berlin, 1871.

ᶜ L. F. Bobertag. Geschichte des Romans und der ihm verwandten Dichtungsgattungen in Deutschland. Vol. I. : Bis zum Anfang des 18. Jahrhunderts. Breslau, 1877. Vol. II. 1 Breslau, 1879 ; Vol. II. 2 Berlin, 1884.

ᶜ Karl Rehorn. Der deutsche Roman. Geschichtliche Rückblicke und kritische Streiflichter. Köln and Leipzig, 1890.

ᶜ **Helm. Mielke.** Der deutsche Roman des 19. Jahrhunderts. Braunschweig, 1890.

E. de Morsier. Romanciers allemands contemporains. (Spielhagen, Heyse, Freytag, Raabe.) Paris, 1890.

J. Dunlop. The History of Fiction, being a critical account of the most celebrated Prose Works of Fiction from the earliest Greek Romances to the Novels of the present age. 3 Vols. Edinburgh, 1814. 3rd ed. London, 1843. A German translation with numerous improvements and additions was made by **Felix Liebrecht** under the title : J. Dunlop's Geschichte der Prosadichtungen oder Geschichte der Romane, Novellen, Märchen, u.s.w. Aus dem Englischen übertragen und vielfach vermehrt und berichtigt so wie mit einleitender Vorrede, ausführlichen Anmerkungen und einem vollständigen Register versehen. Berlin, 1851.

HISTORY OF GERMAN LYRICS.

Jacob Grimm. Über den altdeutschen Meistergesang. Göttingen, 1811.

ᵖ **Otto Weddigen.** Zur Geschichte des Meistergesangs. Wiesbaden, 1891.

ᵖ **Otto Lyon.** Minne- und Meistersang. Bilder aus der Geschichte altdeutscher Litteratur. Leipzig, 1883.

Ed. Schuré. Histoire du Lied. Paris, 1868. A German translation of this work was published under the title : **Edouard Schuré's Geschichte des deutschen Liedes.**

Eingeleitet von **Adolf Stahr.** 3rd ed. (with a preface by **Oskar Schwebel**). Minden i. W., 1884.

A. Reissmann. Das deutsche Lied in seiner historischen Entwickelung dargestellt. Mit Musikbeilagen. Cassel, 1861.

A. Reissmann. Geschichte des deutschen Liedes. Mit Musikbeilagen. Berlin, 1874.

H. Hoffmann v. Fallersleben. Geschichte des deutschen Kirchenliedes bis auf Luthers Zeit. Hannover, [3]1861.

Ed. Emil Koch. Geschichte des Kirchenliedes und Kirchengesanges der christlichen, insbesondere der deutschen evangelischen Kirche. 3rd ed. 8 volumes. Stuttgart, 1866–1876.

H. Hoffmann von Fallersleben. In dulci jubilo Nun singet und seid froh. Kurze Geschichte der lateinisch-deutschen Mischpoesie. Ein Beitrag zur Geschichte der deutschen Poesie. Mit einer Musikbeilage von **Ludwig Erk**. Hannover, [2]1861.

M. v. Waldberg. Deutsche Renaissance-Lyrik. Berlin, 1888. Secular lyrics of the first half of the 17th century.

M. v. Waldberg. Die galante Lyrik. QF. LVI. Strassburg, 1885. Continuation of the former work. Second Silesian School until the rise of the Anacreontic poets.

Eugen Ehrmann. Die bardische Lyrik im achtzehnten Jahrhundert. Halle, 1892.

HISTORY OF THE GERMAN DRAMA.

Karl Hase. Das geistliche Schauspiel. Leipzig, 1858.

H. Reidt. Das geistliche Schauspiel des Mittelalters in Deutschland Frankfurt am Main, 1868.

E. Wilken. Geschichte der geistlichen Spiele in Deutschland. Göttingen, 1872.

E. Froning. Zur Geschichte und Beurtheilung der geistlichen Spiele des Mittelalters. Frankfurt am Main, 1884.

Otto Brahm. Das deutsche Ritterdrama des 18. Jahrhunderts. QF. xl. Strassburg, 1880.

Otto Rühle. Das deutsche Schäferspiel im 18. Jahrhundert. Dissertation. Halle, 1885.

J. Bayer. Von Gottsched bis Schiller. 3 vols. Prag, 1863.

Rob. Prölss. Geschichte des neueren Dramas. 3 vols. Leipzig, 1881-83. (Vol. III. 1 (1883) : Das neuere Drama der Deutschen bis Lessing.)

W. Creizenach. Zur Entstehungsgeschichte des neueren deutschen Lustspiels. Halle, 1879.

W. Creizenach. Geschichte des neueren Dramas. Vol. I. : Mittelalter und Frührenaissance. Halle, 1894. One more volume will follow.

B. Litzmann. Das deutsche Drama in den litterarischen Bewegungen der Gegenwart. Lectures delivered at the University of Bonn. Hamburg, 1894.

J. L. Klein. Geschichte des Dramas. Unfinished. 13 vols. 1865-1876. Index 1886.

Rob. Prutz. Vorlesungen über die Geschichte des Theaters. Berlin, 1847.

ᶜ **E. Devrient.** Geschichte der deutschen Schauspielkunst. 5 volumes. Leipzig, 1848-74.

R. Genée. Lehr- und Wanderjahre des deutschen Schauspiels. Berlin, 1882.

IX.

THEORY OF POETRY.

THEORY OF THE DRAMA, THEORY OF THE EPOS, ETC.

ᵇ **Chr. Friedr. Alb. Schuster.** Lehrbuch der Poetik für höhere Lehranstalten. Halle a/S. ¹1874, ³1890.

Wilhelm Wackernagel. Poetik, Rhetorik, und Stilistik. (Edited by **Ludwig Sieber.**) Halle, 1873.

Moriz Carriere. Die Poesie. Ihr Wesen und ihre Formen, mit Grundzügen der vergleichenden Litteraturgeschichte. Second edition (re-written). Leipzig, Brockhaus, 1884.

Rudolf von Gottschall. Poetik. Die Dichtkunst und ihre Technik. Vom Standpunkte der Neuzeit. Breslau, ²1869, ⁵1882. Two parts in one volume.

Ernst Kleinpaul. Poetik. Die Lehre von der deutschen Dichtkunst. Entworfen von Ernst Kleinpaul, ausgeführt . . . von **Wilhelm Langewiesche.** Ninth edition. Bremen, 1892. Three parts in one volume.

C. Beyer. Deutsche Poetik. Theoretisch-praktisches Handbuch der deutschen Dichtkunst. Second edition. 3 vols. Stuttgart, 1887.

74

ª **Hermann Baumgart.** Handbuch der Poetik. Eine kritisch-historische Darstellung der Theorie der Dichtkunst. Stuttgart, 1887.

Wilhelm Scherer. Poetik. Berlin, 1888 (edited from Scherer's manuscript and with the help of notes taken at his lectures by R. M. Meyer).

Moriz Schmidt. Aristoteles über die Dichtkunst. Griechisch und Deutsch. Jena, 1875. Greek and German text in parallel columns.

Friedrich Spielhagen. Beiträge zur Theorie und Technik des Romans. Leipzig, 1883.

ᶜ **Richard Maria Werner.** Lyrik und Lyriker. Hamburg, 1890.

L. Chevalier. Zur Poetik der Ballade. I., II. Prag, 1891, 1892.

Gustav Freytag. Die Technik des Dramas. Leipzig, ⁶1890.

Robert Prölss. Katechismus der Dramaturgie. Leipzig, 1877.

Hermann Unbescheid. Beitrag zur Behandlung der dramatischen Lektüre. Berlin, 1890, ²1891.

Rudolf Franz. Der Aufbau der Handlung in den klassischen Dramen. Bielefeld and Leipzig, 1892.

X.

METRE.

A.—OLD GERMAN METRE AND STYLE.

*(The metrical theories proposed in the majority of the works enume-
rated under this head are far from being generally accepted,
hence the letter c had to be prefixed to nearly all of them.)*

ac **Eduard Sievers. Altgermanische Metrik.** Halle, 1893.
With full bibliography.

ac **Eduard Sievers. Metrik der altgermanischen Alli-
terationsdichtung.** In Paul's Grundriss, Vol. II. (1892.)
The theories of Sievers, as proposed in many previous essays,
were criticised in the following pamphlets, to part of which
Sievers has replied in his first-mentioned work.

ac **Hermann Möller. Zur althochdeutschen Allitera-
tionspoesie.** Kiel and Leipzig, 1888.

ac **Hermann Hirt. Untersuchungen zur westgermanischen Verskunst.** Leipzig, 1889.

ac **Andreas Heusler.** (*a*) **Der Ljóþaháttr.** Berlin, 1889.
(Acta Germanica. I., 2.) (*b*) **Zur Geschichte der altdeutschen Verskunst.** Breslau, 1891. (Weinhold's Germ.
Abh. No. 8.) (*c*) **Über germanischen Versbau.** Berlin,
1894. (Schriften zur germ. Phil. No. 7.)

76

[ac] **Karl Fuhr.** Die Metrik des westgermanischen Alliterationsverses. Marburg, 1892.

[ac] **Max Kaluza.** Studien zum germanischen Alliterationsvers. Part I. (Kritik der bisherigen Theorien). Part II. (Die Metrik des Beowulfliedes). Berlin, 1894. Kaluza returns to Lachmann's theory.

[ac] **Rudolf Koegel.** Geschichte der deutschen Litteratur bis zum Ausgang des Mittelalters. Vol. I., 288m, sqq. contains a chapter on 'Der epische Langvers,' in which Koegel endeavours to reconcile Sievers's views with those of his opponents.

[a] **Richard M. Meyer.** Die altgermanische Poesie nach ihren formelhaften Elementen beschrieben. Berlin, 1889.

[a] **Karl Müllenhoff.** De antiquissima Germanorum poesi chorica. Kiliae, 1847.

[a] **Richard Heinzel.** Über den Stil der altgermanischen Poesie. Strassburg, 1875. (QF. x.).

[a] **Otto Arndt.** Uber die altgermanische epische Sprache. (Beovulf. Heliand. Müllenhoff and Scherer's Denkmäler. Nibelunge.) Tübinger Dissertation, 1877.

[a] **Otto Hoffmann.** Reimformeln im Westgermanischen. Darmstadt, 1885.

[ac] **Max Rieger.** Die alt- und angelsächsische Verskunst. Halle, 1876.

[ac] **Hermann Paul.** Deutsche Metrik, in Paul's Grundriss, Vol. II. (1892).

ᵃᶜ **Wilhelm Wilmanns.** Der altdeutsche Reimvers. (Beiträge zur Geschichte der älteren deutschen Litteratur. Heft 3.) Bonn, 1887.

ᵃᶜ **Wilhelm Grimm.** Zur Geschichte des Reimes. Berlin, 1852. (From the 'Abhandlungen der Akademie der Wissenschaften in Berlin vom Jahre 1850,' reprinted in Kleinere Schriften, IV. (1887), 125-341).

ᵃ **Richard M. Meyer.** Grundlagen des mittelhochdeutschen Strophenbaues. Strassburg, 1886. (QF. 58.)

B.—MODERN GERMAN METRE.

Jakob Minor. Neuhochdeutsche Metrik. Strassburg, 1893. Contains a very full bibliography. Excellent.

Oskar Schmeckebier. Deutsche Verslehre. Berlin, 1886. An abridged edition of this book is called: **Abriss der deutschen Verslehre und der Lehre von den Dichtungsarten.** Zum Gebrauch beim Unterricht. Berlin, ²1886. Handy for teachers.

ᵃᶜ **Rudolph Westphal.** Theorie der neuhochdeutschen Metrik. Jena, 1870. Zweite sehr vermehrte und durch eine Übersicht der alt- und mittelhochdeutschen Metrik erweiterte Ausgabe. Jena, 1877.

Friedrich Zarncke. Über den fünffüssigen Iambus, mit besonderer Rücksicht auf seine Behandlung durch Lessing, Schiller und Goethe. I. Leipzig, 1865.

Eduard Belling. Die Metrik Schillers. Breslau, 1883.

XI.

GERMAN CLASSICS AND ANNOTATED EDITIONS.

I.—SERIES OF GERMAN CLASSICS.

(Only the most important series will be enumerated.)

A.—GENERAL (OLD AND MODERN CLASSICS).

Deutsche National-Litteratur. Historisch kritische Ausgabe, herausgegeben von **Joseph Kürschner.** Berlin and Stuttgart. (Abbrev. DNL.)

> Many editors. Some volumes are excellent, others less satisfactory. In progress. The series now amounts to 209 volumes and is not yet completed.

a **Bibliothek des litterarischen Vereins in Stuttgart.** In progress. Stuttgart. Since 1842. A most valuable collection, which contains also very important Romance (Old French, Old Provençal, etc.) texts.

b **Sammlung Göschen. Schulausgaben aus allen Lehrfächern.** Vol. 10 (Nibelungen und Kudrun), 22 (Hartmann von Aue, Wolfram von Eschenbach, und Gottfried von Strassburg), 23 (Minnesang und Spruchdichtung), 24 (Sebastian Brant, Luther, Hans Sachs, Fischart), 25 (Kirchenlied und Volkslied), 28 (Old High German).

> Selections. Excellent and cheap editions for school purposes. The series is being continued.

79

ᵇ Denkmäler der älteren deutschen Litteratur für den litteraturgeschichtlichen Unterricht an höheren Lehr- anstalten, edited by Gotthold Bötticher and Karl Kinzel. Many little vols. (8th to 18th centuries). Halle a/S. Since 1889. Most useful for school purposes.

B.—OLD GERMAN CLASSICS.

(The single numbers of the older series are given in v. Bahder's Grundriss.)

ᵃᶜ Bibliothek der gesammten deutschen National-Litteratur von der ältesten bis auf die neuere Zeit. Abtheilung I. Quedlinburg, 1835-75.

Many of the more important texts may now be consulted in more recent editions, but for others the series is still very valuable. Only the first division contains texts, the second contains essays, the third one glossaries.

Dichtungen des deutschen Mittelalters. Vols. 1-8. Leipzig, 1843-52.

Most volumes were edited by Franz Pfeiffer.

Bibliothek der ältesten deutschen Litteratur-Denkmäler, von M. Heyne. Paderborn. 14 volumes. 1858-77. Many new editions of vols. of this series. For students.

ᴾ Deutsche Classiker des Mittelalters. Mit Wort- und Sacherklärungen. Begründet von Franz Pfeiffer. 12 vols. Leipzig, 1865-81. Frequent new editions. Many translations and explanations under the text.

ᴾ Deutsche Dichtungen des Mittelalters. Mit Wort- und Sacherklärungen. Herausgegeben von **Karl Bartsch.** 5 vols. Leipzig, 1872-77.

A supplementary series to the classics enumerated under the previous heading.

Germanistischer Bücherschatz, herausgegeben von **Alfred Holder.** 10 parts. Freiburg, 1882-84.

Germanistische Handbibliothek begründet von **Julius Zacher.** The present general editor is **Eduard Sievers.** 8 vols. Halle a/S., 1869-93. The texts are accompanied by elaborate introductions, a full survey of the various readings and many critical and explanatory notes. For scholars.

Altdeutsche Textbibliothek, herausgegeben von **Hermann Paul.** 10 vols. Halle a/S., 1882-90. For students.

Sammlung germanistischer Hülfsmittel für den praktischen Studienzweck. Halle a/S. 3 vols. 1882-84.

C.—THE XVIᴛʜ AND XVIIᴛʜ CENTURIES.

Bibliothek deutscher Dichter des 17ten Jahrhunderts, edited by **Wilhelm Müller** and **Karl Förster.** 14 vols. Leipzig, 1822-38.

Neudrucke deutscher Litteraturwerke des 16. und 17. Jahrhunderts. Herausgegeben von **Wilhelm Braune.** Halle a/S. Since 1882. Consists now of 137 parts. Excellent. [Abbrev. :—Braune's Neudrucke.]

Deutsche Dichter des 16. Jahrhunderts. Mit Einleitungen und Worterklärungen, herausgegeben von **Karl Goedeke** und **Julius Tittmann.** Leipzig. Since 1867.

F

Deutsche Dichter des 17. Jahrhunderts. Mit Einleitungen und Anmerkungen, herausgegeben von Karl
Goedeke und Julius Tittmann. Leipzig. Since 1869.

D.—THE XVIIITH AND XIXTH CENTURIES.

Deutsche Litteraturdenkmale des 18. Jahrhunderts. In
Neudrucken herausgegeben von Bernhard Seuffert. Heilbronn, now Stuttgart, 1882-94. 50 Parts. Excellent.

Deutsche Litteraturdenkmale des 18. und 19. Jahr-
hunderts. Edited by August Sauer. Neue Folge. No. 1.
Stuttgart, 1894.
   Continuation of the preceding collection. Excellent.

Bibliothek der deutschen National-Literatur des 18. und
19. Jahrhunderts. Leipzig : Brockhaus. Very. useful.

The Cotta editions of the German Classics. Stuttgart :
Cotta. Most of them also in Cotta's 'Bibliothek der
Weltlitteratur.' To be recommended.

The Hempel editions of the German Classics. Berlin :
Hempel. (Part of this series was re-issued by Fr. Dümmler.)

The editions published by the Bibliographisches Institut.
Hildburghausen, now Leipzig. Partly very valuable.

Collection Spemann. Stuttgart : Spemann. Useful series.

The Hendel editions. Halle. Hendel. Cheap.

The Reclam editions. Leipzig : Reclam. (Reclam's 'Universalbibliothek.') Very cheap.

Meyers Volksbücher. Leipzig: Bibliographisches Institut. The
cheapest series of all.

E.—SPECIAL DISTRICTS.

Bibliothek älterer Schriftwerke der deutschen Schweiz und ihres Grenzgebietes, ed. by Jakob Baechtold and Ferdinand Vetter. Frauenfeld. Since 1877.

Elsässische Litteraturdenkmäler aus dem 14.—17. Jahrhundert, ed. by Ernst Martin and Erich Schmidt. Strassburg. Since 1878. Vol. V., 1888.

Ältere tirolische Dichter. Various editors. Innsbruck. Since 1874.

Bibliothek der mittelhochdeutschen Litteratur in Böhmen, ed. Ernst Martin. Prag. Since 1876. Vol. IV., 1893.

Schlesische Denkmäler des deutschen Schrifttums im Mittelalter, ed. Paul Pietsch. Breslau. Since 1881.

Niederdeutsche Denkmäler, edited by the Verein für niederdeutsche Sprachforschung. Bremen, now Norden. Since 1876.

F.—OLDER TRANSLATIONS.

Bibliothek älterer deutscher Übersetzungen, herausgegeben von August Sauer. Vol. I. Die schöne Magelone, aus dem Französischen übersetzt von Veit Warbek, 1527, nach der Originalhandschrift herausgegeben von Johannes Bolte, Berlin, 1894.

II.

EDITIONS OF SOME IMPORTANT OLD GERMAN CLASSICS.

A.—GOTHIC (WULFILA).

[ac] **H. C. v. d. Gabelentz** and **J. Loebe's** edition in 2 vols. Altenburg and Leipzig, 1836-46.

[a] **Andreas Uppström.** Ulfilas. Upsala, 1854-68. (Several publications. Authentic readings.)

[ac] **H. F. Massmann.** Ulfilas. Stuttgart, 1857. (Gothic-Greek-Latin text, and a Glossary.)

Ernst Bernhardt. Vulfila oder die gotische Bibel. Halle, 1876. With the Greek original. (Germanistische Handbibliothek. Vol. III.)

[b] **Ernst Bernhardt.** Die gotische Bibel des Vulfila. (Sammlung germanistischer Hilfsmittel. Vol. III.) Halle, 1884.

[b] **Friedr. Ludw. Stamm(-Moritz Heyne).** Ulfilas. (Text, Grammar, Glossary.) Paderborn, 1858, [8]1885.

C. H. Balg. The first Germanic Bible translated from the Greek by the Gothic bishop Wulfila in the fourth century, and the other remains of the Gothic language, edited with an Introduction, a Syntax, and a Glossary by C. H. Balg. Milwaukee, New York, London, Halle, 1891.

B.—OLD SAXON.

ᶜ **J. Andreas Schmeller.** Heliand. Poema Saxonicum seculi noni. Part I. (Text) Monachii (Munich), 1830. Part II. (Valuable Glossary), 1840. The readings of the MSS. are not always correctly given.

Moritz Heyne. Heliand, mit ausführlichem Glossar. Paderborn, 1865, ³1883.

Heinrich Rückert. Heliand. Leipzig, 1876. (Short glossary compiled after Rückert's death by K. Bartsch. Useful notes. Deutsche Dichtungen des Mittelalters. Vol. IV.)

Eduard Sievers. Heliand. Halle, 1878. (Best edition for scientific research. Reliable parallel text of the two great manuscripts. Valuable collection of typical expressions. No glossary.)

Otto Behaghel. Heliand. Halle, 1882. (Paul's Altdeutsche Textbibliothek. Vol. I. Handy Students' edition.)

Karl Zangemeister und Wilhelm Braune. Bruchstücke der altsächsischen Bibeldichtung aus der Bibliotheca Palatina. Heidelberg, 1894. (Cf. 'Neue Heidelberger Jahrbücher,' iv., 2, in which photographic facsimiles of the newly discovered fragments are given.)

C.—OLD HIGH GERMAN.

(For Collections of Specimens see page 97.)

(a) OTFRID.

Johann Kelle. Otfrids von Weissenburg Evangelienbuch. Regensburg. Vol. I. : Text und Einleitung. 1856.

Vol. II.: Formen- und Lautlehre. 1869.   Vol. III.: Glossar.
1881.

Paul Piper. Otfrids Evangelienbuch, mit Einleitung,
erklärenden Anmerkungen und ausführlichem Glossar.
Freiburg and Tübingen.   Part I., ²1882 (Introduction, Text,
Notes); Part II., ²1887 (Glossary, Sketch of Grammar, Full
Bibliography).

Oskar Erdmann. Otfrids Evangelienbuch herausgegeben
und erklärt. Halle, 1882. (Germanistische Handbibliothek. Vol. 5.) Text and notes. No glossary. A very
valuable syntax on the language of Otfrid was published by
Erdmann separately in two parts under the title **Untersuchungen über die Syntax der Sprache Otfrids.**
Halle, 1874 and 1876.

Both Piper and Erdmann have published cheap editions of
their texts and short glossaries. **Piper's** edition is dated
Freiburg, 1882 and 1884 (Holder's germanistischer Bücherschatz. Vols. 4 and 11); **Erdmann's** was published at
Halle, 1882 (Sammlung germanistischer Hülfsmittel. Vol. 1).

(*b*) TATIAN.

Eduard Sievers. Tatian. Lateinisch und altdeutsch
mit ausführlichem Glossar. Paderborn, 1872, ²1892.

(*c*) NOTKER.

Paul Piper. Die Schriften Notkers und seiner Schule.
Freiburg, 1882-3. (Holder's Germanistischer Bücherschatz.
Vols. 8-10.)

(*d*) SMALL PIECES.

ac **Karl Müllenhoff und Wilhelm Scherer.** Denkmäler deutscher Poesie und Prosa aus dem 8.-12.

Jahrhundert. Berlin, [1]1864, [2]1873, [3]1892 (in 2 volumes). The third revised edition was edited by **Elias Steinmeyer.** A very important complete edition of the numerous small O.H.G. and O.L.G. pieces with valuable critical notes. Vol. I. : Texts. Vol. II. : Notes. No glossary.

(e) GLOSSES.

Die althochdeutschen Glossen gesammelt und bearbeitet von **Elias Steinmeyer** und **Eduard Sievers.** Vol. I. : Glossen zu biblischen Schriften. Berlin, 1879. Vol. II. : Glossen zu nichtbiblischen Schriften. Berlin, 1882. The collection is not yet completed.

D.—MIDDLE HIGH GERMAN.

(a) NIBELUNGENLIED.

Karl Lachmann. Der Nibelunge Noth und die Klage. Nach der ältesten Ueberlieferung mit Bezeichnung des Unechten und mit den Abweichungen der gemeinen Lesart. Berlin, 1826, [5]1878. (A handy reprint of the text in a small edition. Berlin, [10]1881. This edition is based on the readings of MS. **A.**)

Karl Bartsch. Der Nibelunge Not. Mit den Abweichungen von der Nibelunge Liet, den Lesarten sämmtlicher Handschriften und einem Wörterbuche. Leipzig. Part I. (Text), 1870. Part II. 1 (Various Readings), 1876. Part II. 2 (Glossary), 1880. A school edition, with numerous notes : Das Nibelungenlied. Leipzig, [6]1886. (In Pfeiffer's series : Deutsche Classiker des Mittelalters. Vol. 3. The text is based on the readings of MS. **B.**)

Friedrich Zarncke. Das Nibelungenlied. Leipzig, [6]1887. (The text of this edition is based on the text of MS. C. It has been frequently printed without the learned introduction, for the use of German schools.)

(b) KUDRUN.

Ernst Martin. Kudrun. Halle, 1872 (Zacher's Germanistische Handbibliothek, vol. 2), and a small edition (in the 'Sammlung German. Hülfsmittel,' vol. 2). Halle a/S., 1883.

Karl Bartsch. Kudrun. Leipzig, [4]1880. (Pfeiffer's Deutsche Classiker des Mittelalters. Vol. 2).

Barend Symons. Kudrun. Halle, 1883. (Paul's Altdeutsche Textbibliothek. Vol. 5).

(c) HELDENBUCH.

Deutsches Heldenbuch. 5 parts. Berlin, 1866-78. Critical editions of the texts. The various M.H.G. poems have been edited at the suggestion of **Karl Müllenhoff** by **O. Jänicke, E. Martin, A. Amelung,** and **J. Zupitza.**

[p] **Emil Henrici.** Das deutsche Heldenbuch. Auswahl mit verbindender Erzählung. (Kürschners Deutsche Nat. Lit. Vol. 7.) Stuttgart und Berlin. No year.

(d) PARZIVAL, TITUREL.

Karl Lachmann. Wolfram von Eschenbach. Berlin, 1833, [5]1891.

Karl Bartsch. Wolfram's von Eschenbach Parzival und Titurel. Leipzig, 1870-7. Vol. I[1]., 1871. 3 parts. (Pfeiffer's Deutsche Classiker des Mittelalters. Vols. 9-11.)

. (*e*) IWEIN.

G. F. Benecke und **Karl Lachmann. Iwein. Eine Erzählung von Hartmann von Aue.** Berlin, ⁴1877. With many useful notes. A complete glossary was compiled by **G. F. Benecke.** Göttingen, 1833, ²1874.

Fedor Bech. Hartmann von Aue. III. (D.C.d.M. Vol. 6 : Iwein oder der Ritter mit dem Löwen). Leipzig, ²1873, ³1888.

Emil Henrici. Iwein, der Ritter mit dem Löwen. Halle. (Zacher's germanistische Handbibliothek. Vol. 8.) Part I., 1891. Text and various readings. Part II. Notes, 1893.

(*f*) DER ARME HEINRICH.

Fedor Bech. Hartmann von Aue. II. (D.C.d.M. Vol. 5.) Leipzig, ²1873. (Contains Hartmann's Lieder, Büchlein, Gregorjus, der arme Heinrich.)

Wilhelm Wackernagel. Der arme Heinrich Herrn Hartmanns von Aue und zwei jüngere Prosalegenden verwandten Inhalts. Edited after Wackernagel's death by **W. Toischer.** Basel, 1885.

Hermann Paul. Der arme Heinrich. Halle, 1882. (Altdeutsche Textbibliothek. Vol. 3.)

(*g*) MEIER HELMBRECHT.

Hans Lambel. Erzählungen und Schwänke. Leipzig, 1872. (D.C.d.M., Vol. 12. Helmbrecht is the third of nine stories contained in the volume.)

Friedrich Keinz. Helmbrecht und seine Heimat.
Leipzig, ²1887.

(*h*) LYRICS, BEFORE AND AFTER WALTHER.

Des Minnesangs Frühling, edited by **Karl Lachmann**
and **Moritz Haupt.** Leipzig, 1857. ⁴1888 (by **F. Vogt**)
A complete critical edition of all the songs of all the
Minnesinger before Walther von der Vogelweide.

Die Lieder Neidharts von Reuenthal, edited by
Friedrich Keinz. Leipzig, 1889.

Die Gedichte Reinmars von Zweter, edited by **Gustav
Roethe.** Leipzig, 1887.

ᴬᶜ **Minnesinger.** Deutsche Liederdichter des 12., 13.,
14. Jahrhunderts. Aus allen bekannten Handschriften und früheren Drucken gesammelt und berichtigt,
edited by **Friedrich Heinrich v. d. Hagen,** etc. 4 parts
containing all the songs from all the manuscripts then
known. Leipzig, 1838. (Abbrev. : HMS., or Hagen, MS.)
A fifth part was published under the separate title :
Bildersaal altdeutscher Dichter. Bildnisse, Wappen
und Darstellungen aus dem Leben und den Liedern der
deutschen Dichter des 12.-14. Jahrhunderts. Nach
Handschriften, Gemälden, vornämlich der Manesseschen
Sammlung und nach anderen gleichzeitigen bildlichen Denk-
malen, etc. Berlin, 1856. (Abbrev.: HBS., or Hagen, BS.)

Carmina Burana. Lateinische und Deutsche Lieder
und Gedichte einer Handschrift des 13. Jahrhunderts
aus Benedictbeuern, edited by **Andreas Schmeller.**
Stuttgart, 1847. 2nd edition. Breslau, 1883.

Deutsche Liederdichter des 12.-14. Jahrhunderts.
Selected by **Karl Bartsch.** Leipzig, 1864, ²1879, ³1893
(edited by **Wolfgang Golther**).

Der Minnesang des 12. bis 14. Jahrhunderts.
Selected by **Friedrich Pfaff.** Part I. Stuttgart. No year.
(Kürschner's Deutsche National-Litteratur. Vol. 186.)

Meisterlieder der Kolmarer Handschrift, edited by
Karl Bartsch. Stuttgart, 1862. (Bibliothek des litterar.
Vereins in Stuttgart. Vol. 68.)

(*i*) WALTHER VON DER VOGELWEIDE.

Karl Lachmann. Die Gedichte Walthers von der
Vogelweide. Berlin, 1827, ⁵1875. (A reprint of this
edition appeared in 1891.)

Wilhelm Wackernagel und Max Rieger. Walther
von der Vogelweide nebst Ulrich von Singenberg
und Leuthold von Seven. Giessen, 1862.

Franz Pfeiffer. Walther von der Vogelweide. Leipzig,
1864, ⁶1880 (by **K. Bartsch.** D. C. d. M. Vol. 1.).

Wilhelm Wilmanns. Walther von der Vogelweide.
Halle, ²1883. (The second edition is in every way a new
work. It is the first volume of Zacher's Germanistische
Handbibliothek, and contains a very full commentary.)

Wilhelm Wilmanns. Walther von der Vogelweide.
Halle, 1886. (This is only the text of the poems in a
different order of arrangement, without notes but with a
concise glossary. Sammlung germanistischer Hülfsmittel
für den praktischen Studienzweck. Vol. 5.)

Hermann Paul. Die Gedichte Walthers von der Vogelweide. Halle, 1882, [2]1894. (Altdeutsche Textbibliothek. Vol. 1.)

Beside these editions there exist several selections for the use of schools.

E.—MIDDLE LOW GERMAN (REINKE DE VOS).

Hoffmann v. Fallersleben. Reinke de Vos nach der Lübecker Ausgabe vom Jahre 1498 mit Einleitung, Anmerkungen und Wörterbuch. Breslau, 1834, [2]1852.

August Lübben. Reinke de Vos nach der ältesten Ausgabe (Lübeck 1498), mit Einleitung, Anmerkungen und einem Wörterbuche. Oldenburg, 1867.

Karl Schröder. Reinke de Vos. Leipzig, 1872. (Deutsche Dichtungen des Mittelalters. Vol. 2.)

Friedrich Prien. Reinke de Vos. Halle, 1887. (Paul's Altdeutsche Textbibliothek. Vol. 8.)

F.—HANS SACHS.

Adalbert v. Keller and **Edmund Goetze.** Hans Sachs' Werke. Tübingen. Many volumes. Since 1870. (Bibliothek des Stuttgarter Litterarischen Vereins.)

Edmund Goetze. Sämmtliche Fastnachtspiele von Hans Sachs. In chronologischer Ordnung nach den Originalen. Halle. Since 1880.

Karl Goedeke and **Julius Tittmann.** Dichtungen des Hans Sachs. 3 vols. Leipzig, [2]1883-85. This is an excellent selection from the numerous works of Hans Sachs. Vol. I. : Geistliche und weltliche Lieder (by K. Goedeke).

Vol. II. : Spruchgedichte (ed. J. Tittmann). Vol. III. :
Dramatische Gedichte (ed. J. Tittmann). [Deutsche Dichter
des 16. Jahrhunderts. Vols. 4-6.]

III.

CRITICAL EDITIONS OF MODERN CLASSICS.

(Only the great critical editions of Lessing, Herder,
Goethe, Schiller can be enumerated here ; for others compare Goedeke's Grundriss, 2nd edition, vols. 4 and 5.)

Lessing. **Gotthold Ephraim Lessings sämmtliche Schrif-
ten.** Herausgegeben von **Karl Lachmann.** 13 vols.
Berlin, 1838. Dritte auf's neue durchgesehene und ver-
mehrte Auflage, besorgt durch **Franz Muncker.** Stuttgart.
Since 1886. Vol. 10. 1894. Will be complete in 15 volumes.
Lessing's **Correspondence** has been well edited by **C. Chr.
Redlich** (vols. 20^1 and 20^2 of the excellent Hempel edition).

Herder. **Herders sämmtliche-Werke.** Herausgegeben von
Bernhard Suphan. Berlin, 1877-1893. 32 vols. (Selection from the large edition, in 4 vols. Berlin, 1884-87.)

Goethe. **Goethes Werke.** Herausgegeben im Auftrage der
Grossherzogin Sophie von Sachsen. Weimar. Since 1887.
[Die Weimarische Ausgabe or Sophienausgabe.]

Many editors. Goethe's works, letters and diaries are
being published. **W. v. Biedermann** has published a wel-
come addition, viz.: Goethe's **Gespräche,** in nine volumes,
which are not included in the Weimar edition. The Weimar
edition will be the standard edition. Cf. also **Fr. Strehlke,**
Goethe's Briefe. Verzeichnis unter Angabe von Quelle, Ort,
Datum und Anfangsworten. Darstellung der Beziehungen
zu den Empfängern. Inhaltsangeben. Mittheilung von
vielen bisher ungedruckten Briefen. 3 vols. Berlin, 1882-4.

Schiller. Schillers sämmtliche Schriften. Historisch-kritische Ausgabe. Im Verein mit **A. Ellissen, R. Köhler, W. Müldener, H. Oesterley, H. Sauppe und W. Vollmer, von Karl Goedeke.** Stuttgart, 1867-76. 15 Parts in 17 vols. Schiller's **Letters** are being published in a critical edition by **Fritz Jonas.** Stuttgart. Four vols. are now completed.

The **Hempel Editions** are also very valuable, and also part of the editions in **Kürschner's Deutsche National-Litteratur.**

IV.

SCHOOL EDITIONS OF MODERN CLASSICS.

(*A*) German Editions with German Notes.

Schöninghs Ausgaben deutscher Klassiker mit Kommentar, für den Schulgebrauch und das Privatstudium. Paderborn. F. Schöningh.

Cottas Schulausgaben deutscher Klassiker. Stuttgart.

Velhagen und Klasings Sammlung deutscher Schulausgaben. Bielefeld und Leipzig. Velhagen und Klasing.

Sammlung Göschen. Schulausgaben aus allen Lehrfächern. Stuttgart. G. F. Göschen.

Perthes' Klassische deutsche Dichtungen mit kurzen Erklärungen für Schule und Haus. Gotha. F. A. Perthes.

Nicolais Editions of German Classics. (No general title.) Berlin. Nicolai.

Hölders Classiker-Ausgaben für den Schulgebrauch. .
Wien. Alfred Hölder.

Freytags Schulausgaben classischer Werke für den
deutschen Unterricht. Wien and Prag. F. Tempsky.

Graesers Schulausgaben classischer Werke. Wien.
H. K. Graeser.

(*B*) English Editions with English Notes.[1]

Pitt Press Series. German Classics. Cambridge. University Press.

Clarendon Press Series. German Classics. Oxford.
Clarendon Press.

Hachette et Cie. German Authors annotated ; German
Readers; German Theatre. London and Paris.

Macmillan's Series of Foreign School Classics. London.

George Bell & Sons, Whittaker & Co. 1. Foreign
Classics. 2. Series of Modern German Authors.
London.

Rivington's Series. London.

Rivington, Percival and Co.'s Series. London.

Fr. Norgate's Graduated Series of German Readings.
London.

---

[1] For particulars cf. *K. Breul* in Lyon's ' Zeitschrift für den deutschen
Unterricht.' Vol. viii. (1894), pp. 167 sqq.

Williams & Norgate's German Classics for English Students. London and Edinburgh.

Heath's German Series. Heath and Co., Boston, U.S.A.

H. Holt & Co.'s German Series. New York, U.S.A.

(*C*) French Editions with French Notes.

Hachette et Cie. Classiques allemands. Paris.

Ch. Delagrave. Classiques allemands. Paris.

Delalain Frères. Classiques allemands. Paris.

Garnier Frères. Classiques allemands. Paris.

L. Cerf, Paris, has published the excellent edd. of **A. Chuquet.**

V.

SPECIMENS FROM THE GERMAN CLASSICS.

(*A*) From the Earliest Times to the
XIXth Century.

Wilhelm Wackernagel. Deutsches Lesebuch. Poetry and Prose. Three parts in four volumes. Parts 4 and 5 of the whole work are formed by Wackernagel's History of German Literature (cf. p. 57), and his Old German Dictionary (cf. p. 45). Basel. Most parts have reached a 5th edition.

ᵖ **Heinrich Kurz.** Geschichte der deutschen Litteratur. Mit ausgewählten Stücken aus den Werken der vorzüglichsten Schriftsteller. 4 volumes. Leipzig, 1892 ; 8th, 7th, and 4th editions of the different volumes. With numerous woodcuts. Cf. p. 58.

ᵖ **Max Müller.** The German Classics from the fourth to the nineteenth century. With biographical notices, translations into Modern German, and notes. Oxford, ¹1858, ²1886 in two volumes. (The new edition was revised, enlarged, and adapted to W. Scherer's 'History of German Literature' (cf. p. 58), by **Franz Lichtenstein** and **Eugen Joseph.**)

(*B*) OLD GERMAN.

ᵇ **Wilhelm Braune.** Althochdeutsches Lesebuch. Halle, ¹1875, ²1881, ³1888. Contains a glossary, a short and useful bibliography, but no notes. For University Lectures.

ᵇ **Paul Piper.** Lesebuch des Althochdeutschen und Altsächsischen. Paderborn, 1880. For Students. Glossary, but no notes. For University Lectures. This is Part II. of Piper's 'Die Sprache und Litteratur Deutschlands bis zum 12. Jahrhundert.' Cf. p. 43.

ᶜ **Oskar Schade.** Altdeutsches Lesebuch ; Gothisch, Altsächsisch, Alt- und Mittelhochdeutsch. Mit literarischen Nachweisen und einem Wörterbuche. 2 vols. (Vol. II. being the glossary ; cf. p. 45). Halle, 1862.

ᵃ **Karl Müllenhoff.** Altdeutsche Sprachproben. Berlin, 1871, ³1878. The fourth edition was done by **Max Roediger.** Berlin, 1886. For critical exercises.

G

Karl Goedeke. Deutsche Dichtung im Mittelalter.
Zweite Ausgabe, vermehrt um Buch XII. : 'Niederdeutsche
Dichtung,' von **Hermann Oesterley.** Dresden, 1871.
Useful for private study. One handy volume.

ᵇ **Philipp Wackernagel.** Edelsteine deutscher Dichtung und Weisheit im XIII. Jahrhundert. Ein mittelhochdeutsches Lesebuch. Frankfurt am Main, 1851, ⁴1874.
Glossary, but no notes. For Schools and Universities.

ᵇ **Karl Weinhold.** Mittelhochdeutsches Lesebuch. 1850.
⁴Wien, 1891. Glossary, Notes, Short theory of M.H.G.
Metre.
For Schools and Universities.

ᵇ **Lorenz Englmann.** Mittelhochdeutsches Lesebuch.
4th edition, by **O. Brenner.** München, 1887. Glossary,
Notes, Grammatical and Metrical Introduction.
For Schools and Universities.

(*C*) MODERN GERMAN.

(*a*) POETRY.

Karl Goedeke. Elf Bücher deutscher Dichtung. Von
Sebastian Brant (1500) bis auf die Gegenwart. Aus den
Quellen. 2 volumes. Leipzig, 1849.
Very valuable. Short introductions, various readings.

Adolf Stern. Fünfzig Jahre deutscher Dichtung. Mit
biographisch-kritischen Einleitungen. Leipzig, 1871, ²1877
(umgearbeitete und vermehrte Auflage).
Treats of the time between 1820 and 1870.

Ferdinand Avenarius. Deutsche Lyrik der Gegenwart seit 1850. Aus den Quellen. Dresden, 1881, ²1884.

Theodor Storm. Hausbuch aus deutschen Dichtern seit Claudius. Braunschweig, ⁴1877.

Theodor Echtermeyer. Auswahl deutscher Gedichte für höhere Schulen. Halle, 1836, ³¹1893 (ed. **Herm. Masius**). Arranged according to the difficulty of the poems.

Georg Scherer. Deutscher Dichterwald. Lyrische **Anthologie.** Stuttgart and Leipzig, ¹¹1885.

Hermann Kluge. Auswahl deutscher Gedichte. Altenburg, 1877, ⁵1893 (with the portraits of the poets). For School purposes. Illustrates his Primer of Literature.

Otto Lyon. Auswahl deutscher Gedichte. Bielefeld and Leipzig. No year (1891 ?).

Karl Kinzel. Gedichte des neunzehnten Jahrhunderts. Halle, 1894.

C. A. Buchheim. Deutsche Lyrik. Selected and arranged with notes and a literary introduction. London, 1875, ⁸1892.

(*b*) PROSE.

Adolf Stern. Fünfzig Jahre deutscher Prosa. 1820-70. Mit biographisch-kritischen Einleitungen. Leipzig, 1873.

R. H. Hiecke. Deutsches Lesebuch für obere Gymnasialklassen, enthaltend eine auf Erweiterung des Gedankenkreises und Bildung der Darstellung berechnete Sammlung auserlesener Prosastücke. 5th edition, by **Th. Vogel** and **G. Berlit.** Leipzig, 1883.

Hermann Masius. Deutsches Lesebuch für höhere Unterrichtsanstalten. Part III : Für obere Klassen. 5th edition. Halle, 1889.

(c) DIALECTS.

J. M. Firmenich-Richartz. Germaniens Völkerstimmen. Sammlung der deutschen Mundarten in Dichtungen, Sagen, Mährchen, Volksliedern, etc. 3 vols. and a supplement. Berlin, 1843-68.

" **Otto Bräunlich.** Die deutschen Mundarten in Dichtungen und Sprachproben. Jena, 1879.

Hermann Welcker. Dialektgedichte. Sammlung von Dichtungen in allen deutschen Mundarten, nebst poetischen Proben aus dem Alt-, Mittel- und Neudeutschen, sowie den germanischen Schwestersprachen. Leipzig, 1889.

VI.

COMMENTARIES AND ANNOTATED EDITIONS OF MODERN SCHOOL CLASSICS FOR THE USE OF TEACHERS AND ADVANCED STUDENTS.

Heinrich Düntzer. Erläuterungen zu den deutschen Klassikern. Leipzig. Most of the great classical epics, poems, and plays (the works by Goethe, Schiller, Lessing, Wieland, Herder, Klopstock, Uhland, which are most widely read), are fully discussed. No texts. Each volume can be bought separately. Frequently new editions.

E. Kuenen und M. Evers. Die deutschen Klassiker
erläutert und gewürdigt, für höhere Lehranstalten
sowie zum Selbststudium. Leipzig. No texts.

M. W. Götzinger. Deutsche Dichter. Fünfte Auflage,
herausgegeben und zum grossen Theile neu bearbeitet von
E. Götzinger. 2 volumes. Aarau, 1876-7.
Texts and explanations.

Karl L. Leimbach. Ausgewählte deutsche Dichtungen
für Lehrer und Freunde der Litteratur erläutert. The first
4 parts. 3rd edition. Kassel, 1882-85. Selected specimens
from the classical writers of the 18th and of the first half
of the 19th century, with numerous explanations.
A continuation of this work is 'Die deutschen Dichter der
Neuzeit und Gegenwart.' Cf. p. 104.

C. Gude. Erläuterungen deutscher Dichtungen. Nebst
Themen zu schriftlichen Aufsätzen in Umrissen und Aus-
führungen. Ein Hülfsbuch beim Unterricht in der Litteratur
und für Freunde derselben. 6th—8th ed. 4 parts. Leipzig,
1881-86.

A. Lüben und C. Nacke. Einführung in die deutsche
Litteratur, vermittelt durch Erläuterungen von Muster-
stücken aus den Werken der vorzüglichsten Schriftsteller.
Für den Schul- und Selbstunterricht. . . . Neunte vermehrte
und verbesserte Auflage von **H. Huth.** 3 vols. Leipzig,
1882-83.

Ernst Eckardt. Einhundert und fünfzig ausgewählte
deutsche Gedichte schulgemäss und eingehend erläutert,
verbunden mit einer elementaren Litteraturgeschichte und
Poetik. Wurzen und Leipzig, 1890.

Otto Lyon. Deutsche Prosastücke und Gedichte
erläutert und behandelt. [Die Lektüre als Grundlage
eines einheitlichen und naturgemässen Unterrichtes
in der deutschen Sprache sowie als Mittelpunkt
nationaler Bildung.] Part I. (Sexta bis Tertia). Leipzig,
1890.

Heinrich Viehoff. Goethe's Gedichte erläutert. Third
edition. Stuttgart, 1876.

G. v. Loeper. Goethe's Gedichte. 3 vols. Berlin, 1884-87.

Heinrich Viehoff. Schiller's Gedichte erläutert. Sixth
edition. Stuttgart, 1887. 3 parts in 1 volume.

Fr. W. Valentin Schmidt. Balladen und Romanzen
der deutschen Dichter Bürger, Stolberg und Schiller.
Erläutert und auf ihre Quellen zurückgeführt. Berlin,
1827. New (unaltered) edition : Leipzig, 1865.

P. Eichholtz. Quellenstudien zu Uhlands Balladen.
Berlin, 1879.

R. Dietlein, W. Dietlein, R. Gosche, F. Polack.
Aus deutschen Lesebüchern. Dichtungen in Poesie
und Prosa erläutert für Schule und Haus ; unter
Mitwirkung namhafter Schulmänner. 4 parts. Gera
und Leipzig, 1891. The 5th part by **O. Frick** and **H.
Gaudig** is exclusively devoted to the discussion of classical
plays.

O. Frick und H. Gaudig. Wegweiser durch die
klassischen Schuldramen. Für die Oberklassen der
höheren Schulen bearbeitet. (This is the 5th part of

the before-mentioned collection 'Aus deutschen Lesebüchern.') Vol. I., Lessing, Goethe. Second edition. Leipzig
und Gera, 1892. Vol. II., Schiller, 1893-94. Excellent
for teachers and advanced students.

P. Goldscheider. **Die Erklärung deutscher Schriftwerke
in den oberen Klassen höherer Lehranstalten.** Berlin,
1889. A 'Nachtrag' was published by Goldscheider in
1893. (Elberfield : Programm.)

ᵖ **Heinrich Bulthaupt.** **Dramaturgie des Schauspiels.**
Oldenburg und Leipzig. Vol. I. (Lessing, Goethe, Schiller,
Kleist). 5th edition, 1893. Vol. II. (Shakespeare). 5th
edition, 1894. Vol. III. (Grillparzer, Hebbel, Ludwig,
Gutzkow, Laube). 3rd edition, 1891.

Ludwig Bellermann. **Schillers Dramen. Beiträge zu
ihrem Verständnis.** 2 volumes. Berlin, 1891-92.

Wilhelm Fielitz. **Studien zu Schillers Dramen.** Leipzig,
1876. (Wallenstein, Maria Stuart, Die Jungfrau v. Orleans.)

Kuno Fischer. **G. E. Lessing als Reformator der
deutschen Litteratur.** 2 parts. Stuttgart, 1881. (Discussion of Lessing's chief plays.)

Kuno Fischer. **Goethe-Schriften.** Heidelberg, 1888-90.
(**Iphigenie,** ²1888 ; **Tasso,** 1890 ; **Erklärungsarten des
Goetheschen Faust,** 1889); **Goethe's Faust.** 2 vols.
Stuttgart, ³1893.

Kuno Fischer. **Schiller-Schriften.** Heidelberg, ²1891-92.
(Vol. I. Schillers Jugend und Wanderjahre in Selbstbekennt-
nissen. Vol. II. : Schiller als Komiker. Vols. III. and IV. :
Schiller als Philosoph.)

RECENT POETRY.

P **Karl Leimbach.** Die deutschen Dichter der Neuzeit
und Gegenwart. Biographien, Charakteristiken und
Auswahl ihrer Dichtungen. Frankfurt a/M. and Leipzig.
Since 1893.

. This work, which is really a continuation (forming Vols. V.
and foll.) of Leimbach's 'Ausgewählte deutsche Dichtungen,'
is being published in parts, and is now (Vol. VI. [Vol. X.
of the whole work], part 1, 1894) half finished.

XII.

POPULAR SONGS, BALLADS, HYMNS, PROVERBS, RIDDLES.

A.—POPULAR SONGS.

(*a*) SPECIMENS.

ᵃ **Franz M. Böhme.** Altdeutsches Liederbuch nach Wort und Weise,.aus dem 12.-17. Jahrhundert. Leipzig, 1877.

A most careful and comprehensive collection, with many melodies.

Achim v. Arnim und Clemens Brentano. Des Knaben Wunderhorn.. Alte deutsche Lieder. 3 vols. Heidelberg, 1806-8. New edition. Berlin, 1845-46. A fourth volume containing a general index, etc., was edited by **Ludwig Erck.** Berlin, 1854.

A cheap reprint of the original edition is given in the Reclam Series. There is an illustrated critical edition by **Ant. Birlinger** and **W. Crecelius.** Wiesbaden, 1874-76.

ᵃ **Ludwig Uhland.** Alte hoch- und niederdeutsche Volkslieder. 2 volumes. Stuttgart und Tübingen, 1844-5.

A popular edition in 2 vols. has been published (no year) in Cotta's 'Bibliothek der Weltlitteratur,' with an introduction by **H. Fischer.**

K. Haltaus. Das Liederbuch der Clara Hätzlerin. Quedlinburg, 1840. This ed. is Vol. VIII. of the 'Bibliothek der gesammten deutschen National-Litteratur.' Cf. p. 80.

Joseph Bergmann. Das Ambraser Liederbuch vom
Jahre 1582. Stuttgart, 1845. (Bibl. d. Litt. Ver. Vol. 12.)

Karl Goedeke und Julius Tittmann. Liederbuch aus
dem 16. Jahrhundert. Leipzig, ¹1867, ²1881.

Rochus v. Liliencron. Deutsches Leben im Volksliede
um 1530. (Kürschner's Nat. Lit. Vol. 13.) Berlin und
Stuttgart. No year. (1884.)

Heinrich August Hoffmann v. Fallersleben. Die
deutschen Gesellschaftslieder des 16. und 17. Jahrhunderts. 2 parts in 1 volume. Leipzig, ²1860.

ᴾ **Karl Kinzel.** Kunst- und Volkslied in der Reforma-
tionszeit. Halle, 1892. For school purposes.

Heinrich August Hoffmann von Fallersleben. Unsere volksthümlichen Lieder. Leipzig, ³1869.
  Alphabetical enumeration of the first lines of the German
  popular songs, with indication of the name of the authors,
  first impressions, melodies, etc.

Ludwig Erck. Deutscher Liederhort. Auswahl der vor-
züglicheren deutschen Volkslieder. Neubearbeitet
und fortgesetzt von Franz M. Böhme. 3 vols. Leipzig,
1893-94.

ᴾ **A. Matthias.** Das deutsche Volkslied. Auswahl.
For school purposes. Bielefeld and Leipzig. No year.

ᴾ **Georg Scherer.** Jungbrunnen. Die schönsten deutschen Volkslieder. Berlin, ³1875.
  Collected and sifted with taste and critical judgment.

Fr. L. v. Soltau. Ein Hundert Deutsche Historische **Volkslieder.** Gesammelt und in den urkundlichen Texten chronologisch geordnet herausgegeben. Leipzig, 1836.

H. R. Hildebrand. Fr. L. v. Soltau's Deutsche Historische Volkslieder. Zweites Hundert. Aus Soltau's und Leyser's Nachlass und anderen Quellen. Leipzig, 1856.

Franz Wilh. v. Ditfurth. Die historisch-politischen **Volkslieder des dreissigjährigen Krieges** (edited by **Karl Bartsch**). Heidelberg, 1882.

Franz Wilh. v. Ditfurth. Die historischen **Volkslieder vom Ende des dreissigjährigen Krieges bis zum Beginn des siebenjährigen.** Heilbronn, 1877.

Franz Wilh. v. Ditfurth. Historische Volkslieder der Zeit von 1756 bis 1871. 2 vols. Berlin, 1871-72.

ᵃ **Rochus v. Liliencron. Die historischen Volkslieder der Deutschen vom 13. bis 16. Jahrhundert gesammelt und erläutert.** Leipzig, 1865-69. 4 volumes and a 'Nachtrag' containing the melodies (Töne), and the alphabetical Index to the whole work.

Ludwig Tobler. Schweizerische Volkslieder. 2 vols. Frauenfeld, 1882, 1884.

(b) ESSAYS ON POPULAR SONGS.

ᵃ **Ludwig Uhland. Abhandlung über das deutsche Volkslied** (in his Schriften zur Geschichte der Dichtung und Sage. Vols. 3 and 4). Stuttgart, 1866. There is a cheap reprint of this work (2 vols.) in Cotta's 'Bibliothek der Weltlitteratur.'

P **A. F. C. Vilmar.** Handbüchlein für Freunde des deutschen Volksliedes. Marburg, [3]1886. (With specimens.)

b **Karl Kinzel.** Deutsche Volkslieder des 16. Jahrhunderts. Berlin, 1885. A good first survey. Specimens.

P **F. E. Wackernell.** Das deutsche Volkslied. Hamburg, 1890.

B.—BALLADS.

a **Ignaz Hub.** Deutschland's Balladen- und Romanzendichter. Würzburg and Karlsruhe. [3]1860.
A vast collection, from Bürger to the present day. It contains much that is worthless.

G. Wendt. Deutscher Balladenschatz. Berlin, [2]1871. Profusely illustrated.

Deutsches Balladenbuch. Leipzig. Fourth edition, 1866. A good selection with many fine illustrations.

C. A. Buchheim. Balladen und Romanzen. London, 1891. With notes and a literary introduction. (Macmillan's Golden Treasury Series.) Reprinted in 1893.

C. Bielefeld. Ballads of Uhland, Goethe, Schiller. London, [3]1880.

E. Fasnacht. Uhland, Ballads and Romances. London, 1888.

Henry Johnson. Schiller's Ballads. Boston, U.S.A., 1888.

W. Wagner. A book of ballads on German history. Cambridge, 1877.

C.—HYMNS.

a Philipp Wackernagel. Das deutsche Kirchenlied von der ältesten Zeit bis zum Anfang des 17. Jahrhunderts. Leipzig, 1864-77. 5 volumes.

D.—PROVERBS.

K. F. W. Wander. Deutsches Sprichwörter-Lexikon. Ein Hausschatz für das deutsche Volk. Leipzig, 1867-80. 5 volumes.

Ida und Otto von Düringsfeld. Die Sprichwörter der germanischen und romanischen Sprachen vergleichend zusammengestellt von Ida und Otto Freiherrn von Reinsberg-Düringsfeld. Leipzig, 1872-5. 2 volumes.

Karl Simrock. Die deutschen Sprichwörter. Frankfurt am Main, 1846, ⁴1881.

W. Binder. Sprichwörterschatz der deutschen Nation. Aus mündlichen und schriftlichen Quellen gesammelt, nebst sprachlichen, sachlichen und geschichtlichen Erläuterungen. Stuttgart, 1873.

Ignaz von Zingerle. Die deutschen Sprichwörter im Mittelalter. Wien, 1864.

E.—RIDDLES.

Karl Simrock. Das deutsche Räthselbuch. Frankfurt am Main. No year (1850), ³1874. Second Series, 1853. Third Series, 1863.

XIII.

FOLKLORE.

A.—MYTHOLOGY.

ac Jacob Grimm. Deutsche Mythologie. Fourth edition.
3 volumes. Berlin, 1875-78. The fourth was revised by
Elard Hugo Meyer. Vol. 3 contains: Nachträge und
Anhang, and a very full general Index.

ac Wilhelm Mannhardt. Mythologische Forschungen.
Edited by Hermann Patzig. Strassburg, 1884. (Q. F. 51.)

p Friedrich Kauffmann. Deutsche Mythologie. Stuttgart, 1890. (Sammlung Göschen. Vol. 15.) For school
purposes.

ac Elard Hugo Meyer. Germanische Mythologie.
Berlin, 1891. (With full bibliography.)

ac E. Mogk. Germanische Mythologie. (In Paul's Grundriss,
(I. 982-1138. With full bibliography.)

B.—HEROIC LEGENDS, POPULAR LEGENDS,
FAIRY TALES.

Wilhelm Grimm. Die deutsche Heldensage. ¹Göttingen,
1829 ; ²Berlin, 1867 (with many additions by Karl Müllenhoff) ; ³Gütersloh, 1889 (by Reinhold Steig).
110

August Raszmann. Die deutsche Heldensage und ihre Heimat. 2 volumes. Hannover, 1857-8, ²1863.

Karl Müllenhoff. Zeugnisse und Excurse zur deutschen Heldensage. Berlin, 1860. (Reprint from Haupt's Zeitschrift. Vol. 12.)

Wilhelm Müller. Mythologie der deutschen Heldensage. Heilbronn, 1886.

Wilhelm Müller. Zur Mythologie der griechischen und deutschen Heldensage. Heilbronn, 1889.

Barend Symons. Deutsche Heldensage (in Paul's Grundriss, II. 1-64.)

ᵇ **O. L. Jiriczek.** Deutsche Heldensage. (Sammlung Göschen. Vol. 32.) Stuttgart, 1894. For school purposes.

A. Raszmann. Die Niflungasaga und das Nibelungenlied. Heilbronn, 1877.

R. v. Muth. Einleitung in das Nibelungenlied. Paderborn, 1877.

Henri Lichtenberger. Le poème et la légende des Nibelungen. Paris, 1891. With a very full bibliography of the subject.

Albert Fécamp. Le poème de Gudrun. Ses origines, sa formation et son histoire. Paris, 1892. (Published in 1894.) It forms Vol. 90 of the 'Bibliothèque de l'école des hautes études,' and contains a very full bibliography.

Richard Heinzel. Über die Walthersage. Wien, 1888.

Richard Heinzel. Über die ostgothische Heldensage. Wien, 1889.

Ludwig Uhland. Schriften zur Geschichte der Dichtung und Sage. Vols. I. and VII. Cf. p. 16.

p **Gotthold Klee.** Die deutschen Heldensagen für Jung
und Alt erzählt. Gütersloh, ⁴1892.

p **Albert Richter.** Deutsche Sagen. 2 vols. Leipzig, 1871.

p **Jacob und Wilhelm Grimm.** Deutsche Sagen. 2 vols.
Berlin, 1816, ²1865.

p **Ludwig Bechstein.** Deutsches Sagenbuch. Leipzig, 1853.

Adalbert Kuhn und W. Schwarz. Norddeutsche
Sagen, Märchen und Gebräuche, etc. Leipzig, 1848.

Jacob und Wilhelm Grimm. Kinder- und Hausmär-
chen. 2 vols. Berlin, 1812-14, ²1819-22. 3 vols. (Vol.
III.: Learned Notes. This vol. is sold separately); ¹⁰1879.

p **Ludwig Bechstein.** Deutsches Märchenbuch. Leipzig,
1845.

p **Ludwig Bechstein.** Neues deutsches Märchenbuch.
Leipzig, 1856.

p **Reinhold Bechstein.** Altdeutsche Märchen, Sagen und
Legenden. Treu nacherzählt und für Jung und Alt
herausgegeben. Leipzig, 1863, ²1877.

p **Karl Simrock.** Die deutschen Volksbücher. 13 vols.
Leipzig, 1845-67. Selection in 2 vols. 1869.

p **Volksbücher des 16. Jahrhunderts** (Eulenspiegel,
Faust, Schildbürger). Kürschners Deutsche National-Litteratur, vol. 25. Edited and explained by **Felix Bobertag.**

XIV.

HISTORY—HISTORY OF CULTURE—LAWS—CUSTOMS—INSTITUTIONS—ART—ENCYCLOPÆDIAS.

Cornelii Taciti Germania.
Many editions. Some may be enumerated.

(*a*) ed. **Karolus Muellenhoffius.** Berlin, 1873.
Contains also the most important passages of other classical authors about the old Germans. No notes.

(*b*) ed. **H. Schweizer-Siedler.** 5th ed. Halle, 1889.

(*c*) ed. **U. Zernial.** Berlin, 1890.   ·

(*d*) **A. Holtzmann,** Germanische Altertümer, etc., ed. **A. Holder.** Leipzig, 1873.

(*e*) ed. **A. Baumstark.** Ausführliche Erläuterung . . . Two Parts. Leipzig, 1875, 1880.

Geschichtschreiber der deutschen Urzeit, translated by **J. Horkel.** Berlin, 1849. Leipzig, ²1884.

Die Geschichtschreiber der deutschen Vorzeit in deutscher Bearbeitung, ed. **W. Wattenbach.** Leipzig. The 'Zweite Gesammtausgabe' should be consulted exclusively. The orig. ed. was published at Berlin, 1849-53.

H

K. Zeuss. Die Deutschen und ihre Nachbarstämme. München, 1837.

ᴾ **Otto Henne am Rhyn.** Kulturgeschichte des deutschen Volkes. Two vols. Berlin, ¹1886, ²1892.

ᴾ **Karl Biedermann.** Deutsche Volks- und Kulturgeschichte. 3 parts in one volume. Leipzig, 1891.

ᵃ **Karl Müllenhoff.** Deutsche Altertumskunde. Vols. I. (1870), II. (1887), III. (1892), and V. (1883), have been published. Berlin, 1870-92.

Georg Holz. Beiträge zur deutschen Alterthumskunde. Heft I. : Die germanische Völkertafel des Ptolemaeus. Mit einer Tabelle. Halle, 1894.

Gustav Freytag. Bilder aus der deutschen Vergangenheit. 4 parts in 5 vols. Leipzig. Many editions.

ᶜ **Ernst Götzinger.** Reallexikon der deutschen Altertümer. Ein Hand- und Nachschlagebuch für Studierende und Laien. Leipzig, 1881.

ᵃᶜ **Jacob Grimm.** Deutsche Rechtsalterthümer. Göttingen, 1828, ²1854, ³1881. (The second and third editions are mere reprints of the first.)

ᵃ **Felix Dahn.** Urgeschichte der germanischen und romanischen Völker. 4 Vols. Berlin, 1880-89.

F. C. Dahlmann (—G. Waitz). Quellenkunde der deutschen Geschichte. Quellen und Bearbeitungen systematisch und chronologisch verzeichnet. Sixth edition by E. Steindorff. Göttingen, 1894.

G. Waitz. Deutsche Verfassungsgeschichte. Vols. I.-VIII. Kiel, 1844-78. Vols. I. and II. in a 3rd ed., Vols. III.-V. in the 2nd ed. 1880.

K. Lamprecht. Deutsche Geschichte. Vols. I.-V. Leipzig, 1891-94 (not yet completed).

W. v. Giesebrecht. Geschichte der deutschen Kaiserzeit. 5 volumes. Leipzig, 1855-88. Vols. I.-III., ⁵Leipzig, 1881-90. Vol. IV., ²Braunschweig, 1877.

K. Lamprecht. Deutsches Wirtschaftsleben im Mittelalter. 3 parts in 4 volumes. Leipzig, 1886.

v. Peucker. Das deutsche Kriegswesen der Urzeiten. 3 vols. Berlin, 1860-64.

G. Köhler. Die Entwickelung des Kriegswesens und der Kriegführung in der Ritterzeit. 3 vols and Index. Breslau, 1886-90.

Theodor Schauffler. Quellenbüchlein zur Kulturgeschichte des deutschen Mittelalters. Aus mittelhochdeutschen Dichtern mit Ausschluss des Nibelungen- und Gudrunliedes und Walthers von der Vogelweide. Leipzig, 1892. (Characteristic passages from M.H.G. authors, with a glossary, but without explanations.)

ᵃ **Otto Hartung.** Die deutschen Altertümer des Nibelungenliedes und der Kudrun. Cöthen, 1894.

ᵖ **Jacob Falke.** Die ritterliche Gesellschaft im Zeitalter des Frauencultus. Berlin. No year.

ᵃ **Karl Weinhold.** Die deutschen Frauen in dem Mittel-alter. Two vols. Wien, 1852, ²1882.
No illustrations. Scientific and interesting.

ᵃ **Alwin Schultz.** Das höfische Leben zur Zeit der Min-nesinger. Two vols. Leipzig, 1879-1880, ²1889-90.
With numerous illustrations. Excellent book of reference.

ᵃ **Alwin Schultz.** Deutsches Leben im 14. und 15. Jahr-hundert. Large edition. Two parts. Wien, 1892. Family edition, abridged. Wien, 1892.

Konrad Burdach. Vom Mittelalter zur Reformation. Forschungen zur Geschichte der deutschen Bildung. Heft I. Halle, 1894.

Ludwig Geiger. Renaissance und Humanismus in Italien und Deutschland. Berlin, 1882.

Alwin Schultz. Alltagsleben einer deutschen Frau zu Anfang des 18. Jahrhunderts. Leipzig, 1890.

Karl Biedermann. Deutschland im achtzehnten Jahr-hundert. Vol. I., ²1880 ; II., ²1880 ; III., 1867 and 1875 ; IV., 1880. Leipzig.

Karl Biedermann. 1815-40. Fünfundzwanzig Jahre deutscher Geschichte. 2 vols. Breslau, 1889-90.

Karl Biedermann. 1840-70. Dreissig Jahre deutscher Geschichte. 2 vols. Breslau, ²1883.

Heinrich von Sybel. Die Begründung des deutschen Reiches durch Wilhelm I. 7 vols. Leipzig, 1889-94.

Wilhelm Oncken. Das Zeitalter des Kaisers Wilhelm. 2 vols. (With numerous illustrations.) Berlin, 1890-92.

c **Le Père Didon. Les Allemands.** Paris, 1884.

Sidney Whitman. Imperial Germany. A critical study
of fact and character. London, 1889. There is a cheap
popular edition of this work.

Paul's Grundriss II., 2. Wirtschaft by **K. Th. v. Inama-
Sternegg;** Recht by **K. v. Amira;** Sitte by **A. Schultz**
and **F. Kålund;** Kriegswesen by **A. Schultz; Kunst** by
A. Schultz and **R. v. Liliencron.**
In the Grundriss further references are given as to the
best literature on the subject.

Geschichte der deutschen Kunst. Various authors.
Five vols. Berlin: Grote, 1885-8.

Rudolf Henning. Das deutsche Haus in seiner historischen Entwickelung. (QF. 47). Strassburg, 1882.

ENCYCLOPÆDIAS.

Allgemeine Encyclopädie der Wissenschaften und
Künste in alphabetischer Folge von genannten
Schriftstellern bearbeitet und herausgegeben von
J. S. Ersch und J. G. Gruber. Leipzig. Since 1818.
Several sections are not yet complete. There are up to now
167 volumes. A-G are complete ; H-Ligatur ; O-Phyxios.
[Abbrev. :—**Ersch und Gruber's Encycl.**]

Meyers Konversations-Lexikon. Leipzig. Bibliographisches Institut. 4th ed. 1885-1890. Seventeen volumes.
In 1891 and 1892 supplements were added. Hence ⁴ 1885-
92, nineteen volumes. A fifth edition is now in course of
publication. Profusely illustrated and thoroughly reliable.

Meyers Kleines Konversations-Lexikon. Leipzig.
Bibliographisches Institut. 5th ed. 1893. Three vols.
Handy and full of useful information.

Brockhaus' Konversations - Lexikon. Allgemeine
Deutsche Real-Encyklopädie. 13th ed. Leipzig, 1882-
* 87. Sixteen vols. A supplementary volume was published
in 1887. Of the 14th ed. (begun in 1892) more than half
is now completed. Excellent.

Brockhaus' Kleines Konversations-Lexikon. 4th ed.
Leipzig, 1888. Two vols. Very useful.

Encyclopædia Britannica. Ninth edition. Especially
Vol. X. (1879) 'Germany.' (The German Language, by
E. Sievers; German History and German Literature, by
J. Sime.) The part containing 'Germany' (part 39) may
be bought separately.

XV.

THE TEACHING OF GERMAN.

(*Most of the books enumerated are intended for German teachers of their native idiom in German High Schools and Colleges. English students and teachers should adapt the matter contained in such books to their wants.*)

C. Colbeck. On the teaching of Modern Languages in Theory and Practice. Cambridge, 1887. Two Lectures.

W. H. Widgery. The teaching of Languages in Schools. London, 1888. With a very useful bibliography.

Michel Bréal. De l'enseignement des langues vivantes. Conférences faites aux étudiants en lettres de la Sorbonne. Paris, 1893.

R. v. Raumer. Der Unterricht im Deutschen. Gütersloh, ⁴1873.

ᶜ **Ernst Laas.** Der deutsche Unterricht auf höheren Lehranstalten. Ein kritisch-organisatorischer Versuch. Berlin, 1872, ed. (by **J. Imelmann**). Berlin, 1886. (With many useful bibliographical references.)

Rudolf Lehmann. Der deutsche Unterricht. Eine Methodik für höhere Lehranstalten. Berlin, 1890. (With many useful bibliographical references.)

Rudolf Hildebrand. Vom deutschen Sprachunterricht in der Schule. Fourth edition. Leipzig und Berlin, 1890.

Stephan Waetzoldt. Die Aufgabe des neusprachlichen Unterrichts und die Vorbildung der Lehrer. Berlin, 1892. Cf. *Educational Times*, May 1, 1894, p. 231.

Methods of teaching Modern Languages. By A. M. Elliott, Calvin Thomas, and others. Boston, U.S.A., 1894. Essays and speeches very unequal in value and importance.

APPENDIX.

A.

LIST OF THE MOST COMMON ABBREVIATIONS USED IN BOOKS ON GERMAN PHILOLOGY AND LITERATURE.

a. =aus
a. =alt, in compounds such as ad. =alt-
deutsch
a.a.O. ; aaO. =am angeführten Orte
abgk. =abgekürzt
abgl. =abgeleitet
Abh. =Abhandlung
AbhAk. =Abhandlungen der Akademie
(der Wissenschaften)
Abkzg. =Abkürzung
abl. =ablautend
Abltg. =Ableitung
Abschn. =Abschnitt
abulg. =altbulgarisch
ad. =altdeutsch
adän. =altdänisch
ADB. = Allgemeine Deutsche Biographie. Cf. p. 64
ae. =altenglisch
AfdA. =Anzeiger für deutsches Alterthum und deutsche Litteratur. Cf.
p. 2
AfLG. = Archiv für Litteraturgeschichte. Cf. p. 5
AfNS. =Archiv für Neuere Sprachen.
Cf. p. 7 *and* ASNS.
afries. =altfriesisch
afrk. =altfränkisch
afrz. =altfranzösisch
agm. =altgermanisch
ags. =angelsächsisch
ahd. =althochdeutsch
aholl. =altholländisch
aind. =altindisch
air. =altirisch

aisl. =altisländisch
Ak. =Akademie
Ak.d.Wiss. =Akademie der Wissenschaften
akelt. =altkeltisch
alat. =altlateinisch
alem. =alemannisch
allg. ; allgm. =allgemein
Alm. =Almanach
an. =altnordisch
andd. =altniederdeutsch
andl. =altniederländisch
angegl. =angeglichen
anltd. =anlautend
Anm. =Anmerkung
Ann. =Annalen
anom. =anomal
ant. =antik, *or* antiquarisch
Anz. =Anzeigen, Anzeiger
Anz.fda. =Anzeiger für deutsches Alterthum und deutsche Litteratur.
Cf. p. 2
ar. =arisch
Arch., A. =Archiv
Art. =Artikel
as. =altsächsisch
ASNS. =Archiv für das Studium der
Neueren Sprachen. Cf. p. 7
Aufl. =Auflage
ausgel. =ausgelassen
ausltd. =auslautend
Ausspr. =Aussprache
AV. =Altertumsverein

B. =Buch, *sometimes* Beiträge

121

bair. = baierisch
BB. = Bezzenberger's Beiträge. Cf. p. 8
Bd. = Band; Bde. = Bände; Bdchn. = Bändchen
Bdtg. = Bedeutung
Bearb. = Bearbeiter ; Bearbtg. = Bearbeitung
Bed. = Bedeutung ; bed. = bedeutet
bef. = befindlich
beil. = beiliegend
Beitr. = Beiträge ; usually short for PBB. which see
Bemkg. = Bemerkung
bes. = besonders
best. = bestimmt
betr. = betreffend
bez. = bezüglich
bezw. ; bzw. = beziehungsweise
bibl. = bibliographisch
Bibl. = Bibliographie, or Bibliothek
bildl. = bildlich
bisw. = bisweilen
Bl. = Blatt; Blätter; Litt. Bl. = Litteraturblatt
BPB. = Beiträge von Paul und Braune ; usually PBB.
br. = brochiert, or breit
Brgm. Grdr. = Brugmann's Grundriss. Cf. p. 23
BSB. = Berliner Sitzungsberichte, short for Sitzungsberichte der königlichen Akademie der Wissenschaften zu Berlin. Cf. p. 13

ca. = circa
cart. = cartonniert
Chr. = Chronik
cymr., kymr. = kymrisch

d. = der (die, das, des, dem, den, etc.) e.g. d. Vf. = der Verfasser
d. = deutsch
DA. ; DAK. = Deutsche Altertumskunde. Cf. p. 114
das. = daselbst
dass. = dasselbe
Dat.d.P. = Dativ der Person
Dat.d.S. = Dativ der Sache

Denkm. = Denkmal, Denkmäler (usually for MSD.)
Denkschr. = Denkschrift
dgl. = dergleichen, desgleichen
DHB., DHb. = Deutsches Heldenbuch
DHS., DHs. = Deutsche Heldensage
d.h. = das heisst
d.i. = das ist
dial. = dialektisch
dicht. = dichterisch
Diss. = Dissertation
d.J. = des Jahres, dieses Jahr
d. M. = diesen Monat, dieses Monats
DLZ. = Deutsche Litteratur Zeitung. Cf. p. 10
DNL. = Deutsche Nationallitteratur. Cf. p. 79
Dr.u.Verl. = Druck und Verlag
dram. = dramatisch
dtsch. = deutsch
Dtz. = Dutzend
DW., DWb., DWB. = Deutsches Wörterbuch. Cf. p. 48

e. = ein, einer (eine, eines, etc.)
ebd. = ebenda, ebendort
ebds. = ebendaselbst
eig., eigtl., eigentl. = eigentlich
Eigenn. = Eigenname
Einl., Einltg. = Einleitung
Einz. = Einzahl
einz. = einzeln
entspr. = entsprechend
entst. = entstellt
ep. = episch
Erf. = Erforschung
Erl. = Erläuterung ; Erll. = Erläuterungen
Et. WB. = Etymologisches Wörterbuch

f. = für, or femininum, or form in compounds, e.g. Grundf.
ff., figd. = folgende
F.f. = Fortsetzung folgt
fg. = folgend ; fgg. = folgende
fl., flekt. = flektiert
Flugschr. = Flugschrift
Forsch. = Forschung
Forts. = Fortsetzung
fries. = friesisch

franz. = französisch
Fussn. = Fussnote
Fw., Fürw. = Fürwort

gäl. = gälisch
gall. = gallisch
GDS., GdSpr. = Geschichte der deutschen Sprache. Cf. p. 27
geb. = geboren, or gebunden
Ged. = Gedicht
ged. = gedichtet
geh. = geheftet
geistl. = geistlich
gek. = gekürzt
gemeingerm. = gemeingermanisch
germ., gm. = germanisch
Germ. = Germania. Cf. p. 2
Germ. Stud. = Germanistische Studien.
Cf. p. 2
Ges. = Gesang, or Gesellschaft
geschr. = geschrieben
gespr. = gesprochen
gest. = gesteigert, or gestorben
gew. = gewöhnlich
G.G., GG. = Grimm's Grammatik. Cf.
p 27
GGA., Gött. gel. Anz. = Göttingische gelehrte Anzeigen. Cf. p. 9
GJ., GJb. = Goethe Jahrbuch. Cf. p. 6
gl. = glossiert; Gl. = Glosse
gleichbd. = gleichbedeutend
gl.N. = gleichen Namens
Goed. Grdr. = Goedeke's Grundriss. Cf.
p. 57
got. = gotisch
gr. = gross
Gr. = Grammatik ; sometimes short for
GG.
Grdf. = Grundform
Grdr. = Grundriss
Gudr. = Gudrun

HB. = Heldenbuch
HBS. = Hagen's Bildersaal. Cf. p. 90
hd. = hochdeutsch
Hel. = Heliand
Hfrbzd. = Halbfranzband
HH. = Herren
hl. = heilig

HMS. = Hagen's Minnesinger. Cf. p. 90
holl. = holländisch
Hptw. = Hauptwort
hrsg. = herausgegeben
HS. = Handschrift ;   HSS. = Hand-
schriften
HS. = Heldensage
hsgb. = herausgegeben
Hsgbr. = Herausgeber
HV. = Historischer Verein
HZ. = Haupt's Zeitschrift. Cf. p. 1

i.a. = im allgemeinen
i.b. = im besondern
idg., idgm. = indogermanisch
ind. = indisch
Inlt. = Inlaut ; inltd. = inlautend
ir. = irisch
Is. = Isidor
isl. = isländisch

Jahrb. = Jahrbuch
Jb. = Jahrbuch ; Jbb. = Jahrbücher
JB. = Jahrbuch, or Jahresbericht
Jb. GdPh. = Jahresbericht der Gesell-
schaft für deutsche Philologie. Cf.
p. 11
Jh. = Jahrhundert ; Jhs. = Jahrhunderts

K., Kap. = Kapitel
KBl. = Korrespondenzblatt
kelt. = keltisch
kgl. = königlich
kgswgs. = keineswegs
Kl. = Klasse
kl. = klein
KL., KLex. = Konversations-Lexikon
Kl.Schr. = Kleine(re) Schriften
km. = keinem ; kn. = keinen
Koberst. Lg. = Koberstein's Litteraturgeschichte. Cf. p. 57
Komm. = Kommentar
Korr. Bl. = Korrespondenzblatt
kymr., cymr. = kymrisch
KZ. = Kuhn's Zeitschrift für vergleichende Sprachforschung. Cf. p. 8

l. = lies
L. = Lied

landschftl. = landschaftlich
LB., Lb. = Lesebuch, or Liederbuch, or Litteraturbericht
LBl., Litt. Bl. = Litteraturblatt
Litt. Bl. f. g. u. r. Ph. = Litteraturblatt für germanische und romanische Philologie. Cf. p. 10
LCB. = Litterarisches Centralblatt. Cf. p. 10
lett. = lettisch
Lfrg. = Lieferung
LG., Litt. G. = Litteraturgeschichte
lit. = litauisch, or literarisch
Litt., Lit. = Litteratur
l. J. = laufenden Jahres
l. M. = laufenden Monats
Lwd. = Leinwand

m. = mit, or masculinum
M. = Mitteilungen
MA. = Mittelalter, or Mundart
Mag. = Magazin
m. B., m. Bed. = meines Bedünkens
MBl., MBll. = Monatsblatt, Monatsblätter
md. = mitteldeutsch
m. E., m. Er. = meines Erachtens
Mehrz. = Mehrzahl
MF. = Minnesangs Frühling. Cf. p. 90
MH., Mh. = Monatsheft
mhd. = mittelhochdeutsch
Mhd. Wb. = Mittelhochdeutsches Wörterbuch. Cf. p. 47
Mhd. HWb. = Mittelhochdeutsches Handwörterbuch. Cf. p. 47
Mhd. Twb. = Mittelhochdeutsches Taschenwörterbuch. Cf. p. 47
mlat. = mittellateinisch
MLN. = Modern Language Notes. Cf. p. 13
mndd. = mittelniederdeutsch
mndl. = mittelniederländisch
m. s. = man sehe
MS. = Manuscript ; MSS. = Manuscripte
MSB. = Münchener Sitzungsberichte. Cf. p. 13
Mschr. = Monatschrift
MSD. = Müllenhoff und Scherer, Denkmäler. Cf. p. 86

MU. = Morphologische Untersuchungen (herausgegeben von Osthoff)
Mus. = Museum

n. = neu, or neutrum ; nhd. = neuhochdeutsch
N. = Notker
N. A. = Neue Ausgabe, Neue Auflage
namtl. = namentlich
Nbf., Nebf., Nebform. = Nebenform
nd., ndd. = niederdeutsch (Nd. Jb. ; Ndd. Forschgn.)
ndl. = niederländisch
NF. = Neue Folge
nhd. = neuhochdeutsch
Nib. = Nibelungenlied
nlat. = neulateinisch
nndd. = neuniederdeutsch
nord. = nordisch

O. = Otfrid
o. = oben ; vgl. o. = vergleiche oben
obd. = oberdeutsch
od. = oder ; rarely : oberdeutsch
ö. or österr. = österreichisch
ogm., ostgm = ostgermanisch
o. O. u. J. = ohne Ort und Jahr
org. = organisch
o. U. d. B. = ohne Unterschied der Bedeutung

PBB., PBb. = Paul und Braune's Beiträge. Cf. p. 8
P. Grdr. = Paul's Grundriss. Cf. p. 19
Ph. = Philologie
pr. = preussisch
Pr. = Presse
Pred. = Predigt
Prgr., Progr. = Programm

QF. = Quellen und Forschungen. Cf. p. 14

RA. = Grimm's Rechtsalterthümer. Cf. p. 116
Ref. = Referent
Rep. = Repertorium
resp. = respective
rglm. = regelmässig
Rh. = Rheinisch

rom. = romanisch
run. = runisch

s. = siehe
S. = Seite
SA. = Sonderabzug, Separatabdruck
Sarsb. = Sarsenetband
SB. = Sitzungsberichte (der kgl. Akademie der Wissenschaften zu . . .)
Schnorr's Arch. = Schnorr's Archiv für Litteraturgeschichte. Cf. p. 5
schw. = schwach, or schweizerisch
s. d. = siehe dieses, or siehe dort
sg., sog. = sogenannt
Sg. = Singular
Sitzgsb. = Sitzungsberichte. Cf. under SB.
skr. = sanskrit
s.o. = siehe oben
Sp. = Spalte
spr. = sprich
Spr. = Sprache, Sprachforschung, or Spruch
st. = stark ; stm. = starkes Masculinum, stf. = starkes Femininum, stn. = starkes Neutrum
St. = Stamm
Steig. = Steigerung
s. u. = siehe unten
s. v. a., s. v. w. = so viel als, so viel wie
sw., schw. = schwach; swm. = schwaches Masculinum, swf. = schwaches Fem., swn. = schwaches Neutrum
s. Z. = seiner Zeit

T. = Tatian
Tb. = Taschenbuch
TBl. = Tageblatt
Term. techn. = Terminus technicus, Kunstausdruck
teilw. = teilweise
Th. = Thema

u. = und
u. a. = unter anderm, or und andere
u. a. O. = und an andern Orten
u. a. m. = und anderes mehr
u. ä. = und ähnliche(s)
übhpt. = überhaupt
übtrgn. = übertragen

ugbdn. = ungebunden
ugm. = urgermanisch
umged. = umgedeutet
umgel. = umgelautet
umgest. = umgestellt
Umschrbg. = Umschreibung
unbel. = unbelegt
unbest. = unbestimmt
unfl. = unflektiert
unorg. = unorganisch
unreg., ureglm. = unregelmässig
u. ö. = und öfter
uridg. = urindogermanisch
Urk. = Urkunde
urnord., unord. = urnordisch
urspr. = ursprünglich
u. s. f., u. s. w. = und so fort, und so weiter
u. v. a. = und viele andere

v. = von
V. = Vers
Vb. = Verb
Vbdg. = Verbindung
verb. = verbessert
verd. = verderbt or verdoppelt
vereinf. = vereinfacht
Verf., Vf. = Verfasser
verfl. J. = verflossenen Jahres
vergr. = vergriffen
verk. = verkürzt
verl. = verlängert
Verl. = Verlag, Verleger
verm. = vermehrt
versch. = verschieden
verschr. = verschrieben
verst. = verstärkt, verstärkend, or verstorben
verw. = verwandt
Vf., Verf. = Verfasser
vgl. = vergleiche, vergleichend (e.g. Zs.f. vgl. Spr.)
viell. = vielleicht
vielm. = vielmehr
v. J. = voriges Jahr, vorigen Jahres, or vom Jahre
Vjs. = Vierteljahrschrift
VLG. = Vierteljahrschrift für Litteraturgeschichte. Cf p. 5

126   HANDY BIBLIOGRAPHICAL GUIDE

v.o. = vergleiche oben
Volksl. = Volkslied
vor. = vorig
vorahd. = voralthochdeutsch
vorgm. = vorgermanisch
v.u. = von unten

.

Wackern. = Wackernagel
wal. = wallsisch
Wb. = Wörterbuch ;   Wbb. = Wörter-
bücher
Wbd. = Wortbildung
Wbdtg. = Wortbedeutung
WBl. = Wochenblatt
wgm. = westgermanisch
Weim. Jb. = Weimarisches   Jahrbuch.
Cf. p. 4
W. KL. = Wackernagel's   Kirchenlied.
Cf. p. 108
Wolfr. = Wolfram von Eschenbach
WSB. = Wiener Sitzungsberichte, *viz.*
Sitzungsberichte der Wiener Akade-
mie der Wissenschaften. Cf. p. 13.
Wz. = Wurzel

z. = zu
Z. = Zeile
z.B. = zum Beispiel
Zbl. = Zauberlied
Zbspr. = Zauberspruch
z.d.St. = zu der Stelle, zu dieser Stelle
z.E. = zum Exempel
Zf. ; Zs.f. = Zeitschrift für

ZfdA., Zs.fda., ZDA. = Zeitschrift für
das deutsche Alterthum. Cf. p. 1
ZfdPh., Zs.fdph., ZDPh. = Zeitschrift
für deutsche Philologie. Cf. p. 2
ZfddU., ZfdU., Zs.fdu., ZDU. = Zeitschrift für den deutschen Unterricht.
Cf. p. 7
Zfddspr., ZfdSpr., Zs.fdspr. = Zeit-
schrift für die deutsche Sprache. Cf.
p. 3
ZföGymn. = Zeitschrift für die öster-
reichischen Gymnasien
ZfprGymn. = Zeitschrift für die preus-
sischen Gymnasien
ZfvglSpr. = Zeitschrift für vergleichende
Sprachforschung. Cf. p. 8
Zg., Ztg. = Zeitung
Zs., Ztschr. = Zeitschrift
zsgs. = zusammengesetzt
zsgz. = zusammengezogen
z.s.Z. = zu seiner Zeit
z.T. = zum Teil
Ztg. = Zeitung ; Ztgg., Ztgn. = Zeitun-
gen
Ztw. = Zeitwort
zus. = zusammen
Zus. = Zusammensetzung
Zuss. = Zusammensetzungen
Zusstzg. = Zusammensetzung
zuw. = zuweilen
zw. = zwischen
Zw., Zeitw. = Zeitwort
z.Z. = zur Zeit
ZZ. = Zacher's Zeitschrift (für deutsche
Philologie). Cf. p. 2

B.

SYMBOLS USED IN BOOKS ON GERMANIC AND GERMAN GRAMMAR.

* The asterisk denotes a hypothetical form which does not occur in any written document, but the existence of which must be assumed on philological grounds. Thus Got. *dôjan* is supposed to stand for older * *dôwjan* ; the M.H.G. *tier* must be traced back to * *dheusó* ; or *Met* to Indgmc. * *medhu.*

√ This symbol is sometimes used to denote the root (Wz.) of a word. It has been adopted from mathematical works, *e.g.* N.H.G. *recht*, M.H.G. O.H.G. *reht*, Gmc. * *rehta*, seems to be an orig. past partic. belonging to the √*rḗǵ-* 'to rule.' Or *Minne*, O.H.G. *minna*, must be traced back to the Gmc. and Indogmc. √*man* or √*men*, ' to think.'

< This symbol, imitating the point of an arrow (←), denotes '(arose) from,' *e.g.* N.H.G. *schwören* < M.H.G. *swern* < O.H.G. *sweren*, *swerjan* ; or N.H.G. *süss* < M.H.G. *süeze* < O.H.G. *suozi* (for *swuozi*) < Gmc. * *swôtu-* < Indogmc. * *swâd-ú.*

> is the opposite of the preceding symbol (from →) and denotes ' became' or ' whence,' *e.g.* O.H.G. *altiro* > M.H.G. *eltere, elter* > N.H.G. *älter* ; O.H.G. *ubil* > M.H.G. *übel*.[1]

: denotes 'rimes with' or 'riming with,' *e.g. Zeiten : Freuden : Leiden :* ; Schiller has *Menschen : wünschen.*

Words, or parts of words, included in [ ]—or printed in Italics while the rest is given in ordinary type—are not found in the мss. or printed books, but must be supplied, *e.g.* daz frôno ch[rûci] *or* daz frôno chrûci.

ṵ, ọ, ạ, ẹ, ị. The dot under unaccented final vowels before a vowel of the next word, or under an unaccented initial vowel following a final vowel, indicates, in old German texts, that such vowel does not form a special syllable, *e.g.* from Otfrid : *diurị arunti* ; *si ịmo* ; or from the Nibelungenlied : *des ẹnkunde* ; *dô gâben sị im ze miete* ; etc.

---

[1] It should, however, be noted that a few scholars use these symbols in the opposite sense, taking < (the symbol for a stream becoming a river) to indicate the development from a primitive to a later form, *e.g. wurdi* < *würde*. But these scholars are in a very small minority. Cf. *Litt. Bl.* 1892, pp. 40, 67, 112, 182, and *PBB.* XVI. (1892), 566.

A.—INDEX OF SUBJECTS.

B.—INDEX OF AUTHORS.

I

ADDENDA